Imprisoned

Sociology of Race and Ethnicity

Imprisoned

Interlocking Oppression in Law Enforcement, Housing, and Public Education

Cassi A. Meyerhoffer

AND

Brittany Leigh Rodriguez

The University of Georgia Press

ATHENS

Athens, Georgia 30602
www.ugapress.org

Set in 10.5/13.5 Garamond Premier Pro Regular
by Manila Typesetting Company

Most University of Georgia Press titles are
available from popular e-book vendors.

Printed digitally

Library of Congress Cataloging-in-Publication Data

Names: Meyerhoffer, Cassi A., author. | Rodriguez, Brittany Leigh, author.
Title: Imprisoned : interlocking oppression in law enforcement, housing, and public education / Cassi A. Meyerhoffer and Brittany Leigh Rodriguez.
Description: Athens : The University of Georgia Press, [2023] | Series: Sociology of race and ethnicity | Includes bibliographical references and index. |
Identifiers: LCCN 2022051884 (print) | LCCN 2022051885 (ebook) | ISBN 9780820364230 (paperback) | ISBN 9780820364223 (hardback) | ISBN 9780820364254 (pdf) | ISBN 9780820364247 (epub)
Subjects: LCSH: African Americans—Social conditions. | African Americans—Economic conditions. | Racism—United States. | Discrimination in housing—United States. | Discrimination in education—United States. | Discrimination in criminal justice administration—United States.
Classification: LCC E185.61 .M584 2023 (print) | LCC E185.61 (ebook) | DDC 305.896/073—dc23/eng/20221110
LC record available at https://lccn.loc.gov/2022051884
LC ebook record available at https://lccn.loc.gov/2022051885

CONTENTS

ACKNOWLEDGMENTS vii

INTRODUCTION 1

CHAPTER 1. Slavery and the Social Construction of Race 12

CHAPTER 2. Slave Patrols and Early Law Enforcement 20

CHAPTER 3. The Great Migration and Early Housing Segregation 30

CHAPTER 4. Contemporary Racial-Residential Segregation 41

CHAPTER 5. Whitewashed, Segregated Education 51

CHAPTER 6. Policing the Ghetto 66

CHAPTER 7. The Contemporary Police State 79

CHAPTER 8. Black Liberation, the Abolition Movement, and Where We Go from Here 92

WORKS CITED 109

INDEX 125

ACKNOWLEDGMENTS

I did not realize this would be the most difficult part of the book to write. No one accomplishes anything on their own and so many people have contributed to the writing of this book that attempts to acknowledge all of them feels nearly impossible.

This book started as a pipe dream on a sunny day in a swimming pool with Jennifer Hernandez, and it finally became a reality when David Brunsma, one of the editors of this series, reached out to me in the fall of 2018 and asked what I was working on. I was about to apply for my fall 2019 sabbatical, so I sent him my book proposal and we set the project in motion. I spent my sabbatical working on the book with plans to finish during spring 2020, but the Coronavirus had different plans. While lockdown may have been a productive time for some, I was home with my partner (also an educator), a three-year-old who had just started virtual pre-school, and a six-year-old who was doing online schooling as well. My partner and I were managing our own classes while trying to keep our children from completely melting down from too much time in a virtual classroom. Needless to say, I didn't get much time to write, reflect, or read. Prior to the shutdown, I had the tremendous pleasure of having my co-author, Brittany Rodriguez, in a graduate course I was teaching on race and racism. By the end of that semester, Brittany had agreed to do a research internship with me the following fall. While I was still working from home, wrangling children and online teaching, Brittany spent fall 2020 working on this book with me on top of her other responsibilities. By the end of the semester, I was so impressed with the volume and quality of work that she had produced that I offered to name her as a co-author on the book. She agreed, and to my delight, wanted to stay on the project until it was finished. I must express my undying gratitude to Brittany for being my partner on this project. She is organized in ways I could only dream of: she is thoughtful, a productive writer, and deeply committed to undoing systems of racism and injustice in the United States. Brittany, I could not have done this without you.

Of course, thank you to the publishing team for this book: Celia Braves, David Brunsma, David Embrick, Paul Grindrod, Mick Gusinde-duffy, Lea Johnson, Zubin Meer, and Bethany Snead. Thank you to everyone on the series advisory board as well: Margaret Abraham, Elijah Anderson, Eduardo Bonilla-Silva, Philomena Essed, James Fenelon, Evelyn Nakano Glenn, Tanya Golash-Boza, David Theo Goldberg, Patricia Hill Collins, José Itzigsohn, Amanda Lewis, Michael Omi, Victor Rios, and Mary Romero.

Thank you to Robert Adelman, Clarke Gocker, MiAsia Harris, and Rachel Jeffrey for reading book proposals and earlier drafts of this manuscript.

Thank you to all my students—you have made me a better scholar, a better anti-racist educator, and a better person. It is for you that I continue doing this work. Special thanks to Margarita Alvarez, Ajenae Amos, Tatyana Andre, Imani Arthurton, Kyle Augustine, Mekhi Barnett, Amari Bell, Kjell Beilman, Jasmine Williams-Bottoms, Anya Boyd, Yenesis Brito, Donte Brooks, Pamela Brooks, Taya Campbell, Agape Cogswell, Emily Collins, Jonah Craggett, Eternity Crnkovic, Jakaya Crump, Patricia Cruz, Renea Dacosta, Earl Davis, Kayla Dayle, Kerry Decker, Rebecca Deotte, Weethne Dorvil, Michael Downes, Asza Dupree, Alyssa Eckstein, Tyler Evans, Steven Fabrizi, Kelly Farrell, Madison Featherston, Shaniqua Fuller, Carlos Galicia, Michelle Gjuraj, Kyle Granello, Yesenia Hernandez, Reginald Hilliard, Antoney Holmes, Tatiana Jackson, Sara Jacobowitz, Renick Jeune, Catherine Johnson, Chaylor Johnson, Kayli Johnson, Sarah Johnson, Tikuan Johnson, Jenisse Kovak, Rock-Edens Lamour, Isaiah Likely, Sarah Lombardi, Daymary Lopez, Michelle Lundstrom, Jazmyn Martinez, Sadiyya Martinez, Morgan McClain, Luciana McClure, Omena McCoy, Special Moore, Jenese Morgan, Olivia Nolen, Tara O'Neil, Abdul Osmanu, Mariam Osmanu, Danyel Oxley, Teree Perkins, Leslie Phang, Aliz Quinones, Brittany Rodriguez, Syed Rizvi, Diana Roman, Jude Rousseau, Skyla Seamans, Erica Shaw, Brianna Smith, Ciara Thomas, Nikeila Thompson, Ametrues Trotman, Gabrielle Trotman, Eghosa Ugbo, Sterling White, Darriah Woodard, Octavia Wright, Isaiah Young, and Oliver Zephirin. Each of you has brought delight and insight into my job. You have taught me more than I've taught you, for sure. Keep fighting.

New Haven's freedom fighters: Kerry Ellington, Sy Frasier, MiAsia Harris, Ashleigh Huckabey, Ala Ochumare, Amelia A. Sherwood, Sun Queen, and Vanesa Suarez, thank you for bringing me in. I'd follow you into fire.

My dear colleagues/friends/co-conspirators, Rosalyn Amenta, Diane Ariza, Amanda Bertana, Kevin Brenon, Kerry Brown, Greg Cochenet, KC Councilor, Siobhan Carter-David, Jessica Kenty-Drane, Clarke Gocker, Joan Heenan, Jennifer Hernandez, Steven Hoffler, Brandon Hutchinson, Melissa Kondrak, Astrid Eich-Krohm, Rachel Jeffrey, Yi-Chun Tricia Lin, Jack Mack, Kim McGann, Emily Tumpson Molina, Mike Mitchell, Adam Pittman, Jessica Powell, Paula Rice, Nick Robertson, Tim Sentman, Richard Strahan, Catherine Tan, Brett Tassone, Emilie Turner, Janani Umamaheswar, Lindsey Voth, Dillon Vrana, and the entire Racial and Intersectional Justice Group (RIJG) at SCSU, thank you for inspiring me and holding me accountable in this work.

Crystal Roybal Dezember, living alongside you showed me, from a young age, what racism looks like and the subtle ways it can impact a person. I didn't have a word for it at the time, but you sparked my desire to recognize and undo systems of injustice, and I promise you, I will never give up. Your love and friendship got me through the worst moments of my childhood and young adult life. I will miss you forever and your impact will never be forgotten.

My forever-mentors, Robert Adelman, Gina Butters, Kris Ewert, Marjukka Ollilainen, Brenda Marsteller-Kowalewski, and Debra Street, the roles that you have played in my life certainly vary, but the one constant is that each of you has shown me there is no "one" way to do anything when I was socialized to believe otherwise. Each of you has shown me love in incredible and unexpected ways, and if not for every single one of you, I would not be the kind of person who could have written this book.

To my parents, Milo Meyerhoffer, and Tammy and Terry Yates, thank you for your undying support. We don't always agree but you've always had my back. You've never faltered in your love for me, and we're finally getting to a place where we can hear one another. Mom, thank you most of all. You've experienced this world in ways I could never imagine, and you still manage to hold onto hope. You hold people together and love them despite how much it takes from you. You instilled in me my desire to make the world better, my passion for education, my need for independence (sometimes to a fault), and my ability to see vulnerability as a strength. Tara Yates Godfrey (Sipsy, Sissy, Taradacytl, Taka, Robbie), despite being six years younger than me, you have always been my North Star, my guide, and my inspiration. I love you more than you could ever know, and despite all your growth and the amazing woman you have become, you will always be my baby sister. Matt Tipping, you know you've always been like a brother to me. You have always believed in me no matter how big I've dreamed, and I would have never left the nest if not for that support.

To my partner and husband, Aron Meyer, thank you for bringing our babies to me at work so I could nurse them and keep working. Thank you for making warm meals to nourish my body and soul. Thank you for grocery shopping and doing all the day-to-day tasks that I'm terrible at. You've always been my #1 supporter. I never imagined marriage would be like this—you make me laugh like no one else can, you help me work through writing blocks, you make sure I take care of myself, you leave me alone when I need silence and solitude, and you are always there when I'm ready to come back. You are patient and kind and weird in all the most perfect ways. Thank you for sticking with me—with us. I can't imagine a better person to face this world with.

To my children, Owen and Eliot, thank you for showing me what I'm capable of. I never imagined motherhood would involve writing a book with one hand while building Hot Wheels tracks and reviewing homework with the other. You are the strangest, most beautiful people I've ever met and I love you more than you will ever know.

Finally, to all my ancestors, but especially Shirley McGrady Martindale, June Meyerhoffer, and Burdell Tipping, thank you for always being on my side. I hope I've made you proud.

Cassi A. Meyerhoffer

This acknowledgement is in recognition, first and foremost, of Dr. Cassi Meyerhoffer. Cassi graciously extended to me an opportunity to embark upon my first sociological publication, for which I otherwise would not have had the opportunity to propel my post-graduate career. I am filled with humility by the sentiment that Cassi saw in me what I had yet to see in myself during my time at Southern Connecticut State University's graduate program. Working alongside Cassi has been an enlightening experience that has allowed me to gain skills and insight that I will carry with me for years to come. Cassi shaped my experience throughout graduate school and laid the foundation for what has come to be my passion for exploring inequities within systems of housing, race, prison systems, criminal justice, and their intersectionality more generally. There are no words to capture the depth and breadth of my gratitude for the opportunity to share in this journey. I only hope to one day be the sociologist that Cassi is.

I must, of course, extend the utmost gratitude to my mother, Zoraida Valdes, who has been an unwavering source of support throughout each chapter of my journey both to and through higher education. As a Latinx, single parent born and raised in Hartford, Conn., Zoraida instilled in me a great sense of commitment to the world of academia and was a relentless advocate on my behalf in rendering opportunities that set me on my current trajectory. It is to her that I owe my accomplishments and successes—past, present, and future. Quite simply, thank you, mom. It is my father, Victor Rodriguez, Jr. who stressed the importance of remaining a life-long learner by feeding my appetite for knowledge and exploration of the world around me at an early age, an appetite for which I pledge to continue to nourish. My extended family is owed appreciation for their ceaseless support over the years as well, starting with my aunt Wendy Liolis. Titi Wendy has stood alongside my mother to share in the celebration of each accomplishment and held my hand through each setback, always offering me guidance and reassurance for which I would be lost without. My aunt Evelyn Sebastian has played an instrumental role in nurturing my love of learning and, in carving her own path to higher education, she has shown me that education has the power to open a world of opportunities and promise. Though technically an only child, I am surrounded by cousins whom I consider sisters—Alexandria Roche, Kayla Rodriguez, Erica Rodriguez, Christine Rivas, and Zoe Liolis—and, like sisters, they keep me grounded through life's turbulence, propel me forward, and remind me that I am never alone in anything that I undertake. I am honored to be surrounded by such incredible women, for whom I have the privilege of calling family. My dynamic, vivacious family is the single most important support system in my life, all of whom, both named and unnamed, have contributed to my successes along the way by offering unconditional love through each high and low.

I must take a moment to thank Dr. Gladys Colon for showing my family the way to navigate higher education by charting her own course as a first-generation, Latinx, Hartford native and sharing her experience with us. Finally, I'd like to acknowledge Hartford Youth Scholars' (HYS) contributions to my academic successes. I am indebted to this organization and its staff, particularly Anthony Byers, for offering my family the necessary tools and resources to more effectively navigate the education systems that be. HYS came into my life at a time in which the school systems nearly failed me, as they do many young people from marginalized communities, and my hope was beginning to dissipate. This organization served as a gateway and, for that, I am forever grateful.

Brittany Leigh Rodriguez

Imprisoned

INTRODUCTION

> What's so exciting about this moment is that we are recognizing that racism is indeed institutional and structural. . . . It is embedded in the very fabric of this country, and we're trying to figure out ways to begin to initiate the process of eliminating that racism.
>
> —Angela Davis

Over the last several years, the United States has experienced a surge in bystander videos that have captured incidents of police brutality and prejudice directed largely at Black people. Public outrage surrounding police brutality persists as these incidents continue to reach the public eye. As public discourse around police brutality and racial inequality largely centers on specific events, there is a dearth of information within the public discourse about systemic racism and how race and racism pervade every single aspect of American life. The ways in which Black people are often treated by law enforcement are reflective of larger historical racial inequities and injustices that extend far beyond the criminal justice system and intersect with how Black people access housing, occupy public spaces, and are treated in American public schools.

Imprisoned: Interlocking Oppression in Law Enforcement, Housing, and Public Education focuses on contemporary systemic racism as it relates to how the U.S. criminal justice system, housing system, and education system intersect to create a matrix of inequality for Black people. To illustrate the systemic nature of racism in American policing and communities, this book highlights contemporary policies and practices that intersect with residential segregation and public schooling that continue to affect Black people on a large-scale, structural level—demonstrating the extent to which the U.S. criminal justice system is tied to where people live and how they are treated and educated in public schools.

This book focuses on the relationships between law enforcement, housing, and public education with respect to the ways in which these systems intersect and have an impact on how Black people are perceived and policed in the United States. We document the connection between policing, housing, and education as well as discuss the ways in which the historical and continued mischaracterization of Black neighborhoods and people has harmed and continues to harm Black people, regardless of whether they live in or have lived in poor, segregated neighborhoods. Criminal justice policy, both past and present, and the characterization of Black people are linked to housing and education in the following ways: (1) characterizations of the "ghetto" transcend the boundaries of any actual, physical "ghetto" and affect how Black people are treated in all spaces; (2) neighborhoods in the United States remain segregated by race and as such, public schools remain segregated, thus increasing the concentrations of poverty and racial groups in our public schools—helping to fuel the school-to-prison pipeline and contribute to the policing of Black children; (3) limited access to jobs, opportunity, and well-funded schools exacerbate existing stereotypes about Black people—impacting how all Black people are perceived by police and thus treated by our criminal justice system regardless of levels of participation in actual criminal acts; and 4) the hypersegregation of Black people in poor communities leaves them more vulnerable to predatory policing policies that they have limited political power to combat.

This book is a sociohistorical project that uses existing critical literatures to link the multiple institutions, policies, and ideologies that contribute to systemic racism. We use existing literatures about the distinct systems of education, housing, and policing, to show how these structures are interconnected to create a matrix of inequality that consistently and intentionally oppresses and marginalizes Black Americans. This work serves to bring forth the historical underpinnings of racial inequalities by way of addressing intersecting subsystems of racism as a means of illuminating just how very layered and all-encompassing American racism is. While many authors focus on one or two components of systemic racism, such as the penal or criminal justice system, this book works to address a range of components to demonstrate how intricately these systems are entangled. In doing so, we illustrate the larger picture as to how these systems are not singular entities, but rather pieces of a greater whole.

Early Criminal Justice Policy

Tensions between law enforcement and people of color is nothing new. Some scholars contend that the first police forces in the United States (called slave patrols in the early 18th century), were created to control fugitive slaves (e.g., Dyson 2017). The issues we see in our criminal justice system are not the product of individual "bad" police officers, but rather the result of an entire system grounded in a racism shaped by intentional historical forces. Without understanding the mechanisms by which racism operates systemically in America, it is impossible to think beyond the narrative of individual acts by single police officers or the individual choices or work ethic of American citizens.

As debates rage on about the Black Lives Matter movement, the existence of racism in America, and the hegemonic rhetoric of color blindness, one thing has remained constant—the systemic disenfranchisement of people of color in the United States. To understand the contemporary treatment of people of color in this country by law enforcement, we must first contextualize the practices and foundations on which contemporary racism was built—something we do extensively throughout this book. The White supremacist racial narrative that created the presumption of guilt for people of color in the United States has shaped every single institution of American society. The narrative of racial difference has polluted the thinking of all Americans. The internalization of the social construction of racial difference affects how Americans think, act, and police one another.

Neighborhoods

While scholars often critique the criminal justice system as the presumed hub of racial inequality and systemic racism, it is not the only area in which systemic racial discrimination occurs. The neighborhoods in which individuals and families live is one of the most determining factors of social mobility and an area rife with individual and institutional levels of discrimination. Until the early 1990s, little scholarly attention was given to racial-residential segregation as a source of racial inequality. However, the publication of Douglas Massey and Nancy A. Denton's *American Apartheid* (1993) was one of the first works to highlight the injustices embedded within our housing and lending institutions—policies that date back to the Great Migration. Massey and Denton address the ways in which the intentional actions of White people led to the racial-residential segregation that continues to plague American cities. Scholars, thereafter, have explored the outcomes of segregation, the forces that created modern ghettos, and the factors that sustain them. In American metropolitan areas, segregation amplifies and exacerbates social and economic problems, leaving African Americans not only disadvantaged economically but often concentrated in poor neighborhoods that are cut-off from economic and educational opportunities as well as social mobility (Massey and Denton 1988, 1993; Wilkes and Iceland 2004). It was not any one policy that led to the segregation of American neighborhoods, but rather a series of policies and laws enacted by our government. Federal, state, and local governments used public-housing policy, redlining, blockbusting, and other banking and lending regulations to purposely segregate every metropolitan area in the nation. These policies, along with historical factors such as industrialization and subsequent deindustrialization, led to the creation of modern ghettos.

The implications of this extend far beyond where one can live. Perceptions of those who live in so-called ghetto neighborhoods are not "contained" by the physical boundaries of the proclaimed ghetto itself. Perceptions of Black people as "representing" the ghetto affect not only those living in poor, segregated Black neighborhoods (Anderson 2012), but also Black and Brown people more generally.

Education, Racism, and the School-to-Prison Pipeline

As a result of racial residential segregation, public schools in the U.S. are more segregated today than at any other time in the last forty years. Due to limited access to and interactions with Black children outside poor, urban environments, school-resource officers have deficit views of Black children (Maxime 2018). For example, Black children are often perceived as deviant or threatening when exhibiting the exact same behavior as their White peers who are not seen as such. One of the most damaging and pernicious ways that school segregation affects children of color is through the school-to-prison pipeline. The ACLU defines the school-to-prison pipeline as "the policies and practices that push our nation's schoolchildren, especially our most at-risk children, out of classrooms and into the juvenile and criminal justice systems" (ACLU of New York). These are school practices that directly and indirectly push children out of school and onto the path to prison. More importantly, these policies affect not only children of middle- and high-school ages but younger children as well. In fact, Black preschool children are 3.6 times more likely to be suspended than White children for exhibiting the same exact behaviors as their White counterparts (Schott Foundation 2016). A Yale University study found that teachers disproportionately watch Black boys for potential misbehavior in comparison with their non-Black peers. Additionally, Black girls as young as six or seven have been criminalized and arrested in public schools for exhibiting behaviors that are consistent with White peers and appropriate for their age group (D'Arcy 2012; Morris 2018). The very nature of these policies reveals the extent to which intentional and systemic racism persists throughout this country as well as the degree to which Black people, including Black children, are policed in public spaces.

It is not only policing that negatively affects children of color in schools, however; Black children in American schools and especially those living in segregated Black neighborhoods receive subpar education in a number of ways. First, the curricula they receive is predominantly White and European from a European pedagogical perspective. Second, these whitewashed curricula are taught to them predominantly by White women who often have deficit views of children of color (due, in part, to housing segregation), which results in hostile environments for Black children, unchecked microaggressions, and less mentorship and support of Black students. Third, because neighborhoods are segregated by race and socioeconomic status, so are public schools—public schools that are often funded by property taxes leaving fewer resources in poor Black schools in the form of guidance counselors, social workers, and nurses.

Policing Blackness

Depictions of Black people, especially Black men, have changed dramatically since slavery. While Black men were characterized as docile and happy during slavery in an attempt to control them, these depictions also carried the connotation that slavery was the best position for Black people (Smiley and Fakunle 2016). However, during reconstruction, as free Black people attempted to occupy spaces previously reserved for White people, compliant and submissive depictions shifted to characterizing Black men as dangerous and especially threatening to White women. The characterizing of Blackness as dangerous seemingly justified the extrajudicial lynching of Black people and served as a way to control and strike fear into the entire Black community (Litwack 2004). Of course, these early characterizations of Black people as dangerous have only become more entrenched in U.S. culture (Alexander 2010; Muhammad 2010) and gave rise to the War on Drugs, zero tolerance drug policies, and continue to justify the disproportionate sentencing of Black people in the minds of many Americans (Alexander 2010). The U.S. narrative of "Blackness as criminal" impacts how Black people are treated in public and private spheres, how they are treated by educators, how they access housing, how they are policed, and how we make decisions about police accountability during moments excessive force, brutality, and police misconduct.

When residential segregation is coupled with stereotypes about Black people, Black neighborhoods, and Black criminality, we are left with a culture in which Black people are overpoliced, treated more harshly by the criminal justice system, and rarely characterized as victims when police use excessive force. The following diagram summarizes the degree to which American systems of policing work individually and collectively to uphold White supremacy in the United States.

Related Work

Jerome Skolnick's *Justice without Trial* (1966) was one of the first attempts to examine the link between policing, perception, and race. Since then, there have been numerous attempts by sociologists, criminologists, and other kinds of scholars to examine police practices, trends in offending, and rates of incarceration. Recently, these tensions have taken on a dramatic urgency. Michelle Alexander, in her groundbreaking book *The New Jim Crow: Mass Incarceration in the Age of Colorblindness* (2010), argues that the contemporary disproportionate mass incarceration of Black and Brown people is essentially a New Jim Crow. This work is important in illustrating the structural similarities and outcomes between Jim Crow segregation in the South and contemporary mass incarceration. Alexander (2010) traces the historical roots of Jim Crow segregation to the so-called War on Drugs and mass incarceration of Black and Brown people, all the while pointing out the systemic factors that allow for the upholding of a racial-caste system that nonetheless bellows sentiments of "color blindness." Angela J. Hattery and Earl Smith, in their book *Policing Black Bodies: How Black Lives are Surveilled and How to Work for Change* (2018), shows how the prison-industrial complex mirrors the plantation economy while linking the school-to-prison pipeline and the disproportionate policing of Black and Brown people to the mass incarceration of these same communities. Carla Shedd, in her book *Unequal City: Race, Schools, and Perceptions of Injustice* (2015), documents the real and symbolic harm done to high-school students while in school, as they travel to school, and in their communities. Shedd pushes readers to view schools not only as institutions of education but also engines of social inequality and stratification. The latter objectives are achieved through the criminalization of children, punitive education, and policies such as "school choice" that only serve to benefit White children at the expense of children of color. Several scholars cover these topics in various ways—highlighting discrimination in our housing markets (Charles 2003; Massey and Denton 1993; Rothstein 2017; Taylor 2019), in our criminal justice system (Alexander 2010), and in our schools (Ferguson 2001). Others focus on the systemic nature of racist ideas, stereotypes, and policies that serve to perpetuate and uphold

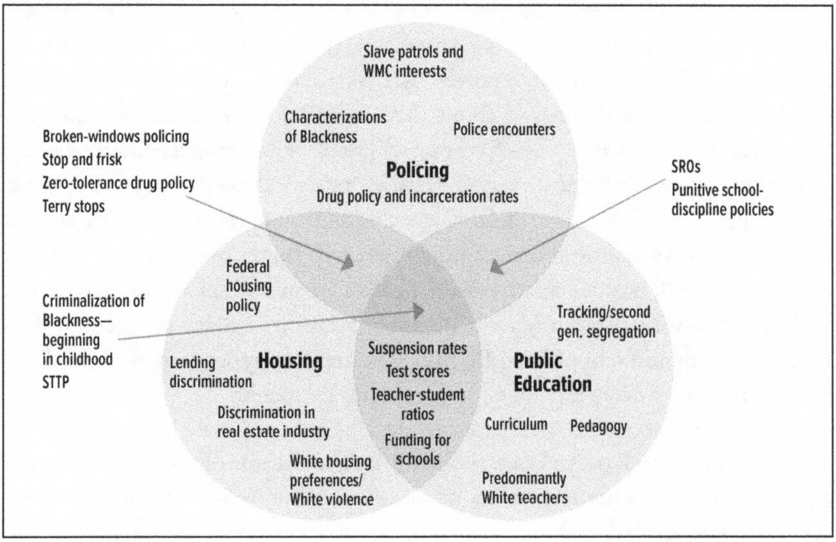

White supremacy (Bonilla-Silva 2014; Feagin 2006, 2010) or how our current system of policing and incarceration mirrors the plantation economy, rates of lynching, and number of people enslaved (Alexander 2010).

Imprisoned is unique in that it explicitly ties together systems of law enforcement, housing, and education, as well as characterizations of Blackness, to demonstrate a matrix of inequality intentionally created to uphold White supremacy at the expense of Black people in the United States.

Book Outline

The first two chapters briefly provide the reader with the historical context in which race and racism first emerged. As a means of justifying the inhumane treatment of Native Americans and enslaved people, differences based on phenotype emerged to distinguish Natives and those who were enslaved from those who were considered White. This early racialization served to establish Whiteness as dominant and normative. Chapter 1, "Slavery and the Social Construction of Race," covers the historical processes of racialization—including the micro and macro factors that shaped and continue to shape racial categorization. Additionally, this chapter problematizes the "real-ness" of race by first discussing the difference between biological and social definitions of race. We cannot understand contemporary racial inequality without, first, understanding how this racial hierarchy came to be. Here, we contextualize the modern-day treatment of people of color by exploring specific historical moments in U.S. history that not only shaped perceptions of African Americans, Native Americans, and Mexican Americans, but also laid the foundation for contemporary race relations in the United States. This chapter ends with a discussion about the construction of Whiteness and how the creation of the White/non-White or white/Black binary perpetuates ideas of Whiteness as normative and everyone else as "other." These distinctions later become especially important as homeowners' associations restrict housing according to race, banks redline entire communities based on the assumption that Black communities will not be lucrative for the banks, people who have come to define themselves as White violently resist the incorporation of Black people into their neighborhoods and schools, and Black people are disproportionately policed and treated unfairly at every level of our criminal justice system.

In chapter 2, we cover the history of slave patrols and early law enforcement. The creation of modern American policing has a multitude of roots, but it is most significantly tied to the institution of slavery and the controlling of Black people. Slave patrols and night watches—the twin ancestors of the modern police department—were created to control and patrol the behaviors and lives of Black and Native populations. In chapter 2, we explore the origins of our contemporary system of law enforcement. Slavery was a major force that shaped early U.S. policing. Southern cities such as New Orleans, Savannah, and Charleston employed uniformed officers who were connected to a larger system of criminal justice (Vitale 2017). The primary function of these officers was to prevent slave revolts, terrorize fugitive slaves, and protect the property of White plantation owners. Because enslaved people with proper permits could work away from the plantation and often fraternized with free Black people, the White population deemed it essential to have heavily armed guards to monitor the Black population. By the Jim Crow era, policing was a central tool for maintaining racial (and class) inequality. Local police worked closely with and were populated by members of the Ku Klux Klan, which we discuss in terms of the role of White supremacy as a persistent pillar of policing.

Chapters 3, 4, and 5 cover the Great Migration, industrialization, and deindustrialization and ensuing White flight/suburbanization, racial-residential segregation, educational inequality, as well as how segregated, whitewashed education disproportionately serves to disenfranchise and criminalize Black children. These chapters will connect early racialization and laws that were established during slavery and Reconstruction to the mass movement of Black people from rural southern states to northern industrial states—paving the way for racial-residential segregation. Most Americans consider residential location to be largely about individual choice and believe the reason White and Black folks live largely segregated from each other is because they prefer to. This way of thinking is premised on the belief that race is biological and that "people want to live with their own." This perspective is shortsighted and lacking in a historical and sociological understanding of how America's neighborhoods have been shaped—not by personal choice but by intentional government policy aimed at keeping Black people out of White neighborhoods. An intentional racial-caste system was created in the United States that positioned White as hegemonic and, therefore, Black was effectively "othered" and marginalized; as a further result, African Americans were intentionally excluded from White neighborhoods and home ownership, more generally.

In chapter 3, we discuss the Great Migration of six million African Americans from southern states to northern industrialized urban spaces between 1910–70—one of the most significant demographic shifts in U.S. history. Fueling this rapid migration was growing racism in the south, Jim Crow segregation, widespread lynching of Black people, and limited social and economic mobility within southern states (Tolnay 2003). Additionally, World War I labor shortages in the northern factories were attractive to southern Black people who had limited economic opportunities. The promise of less race-related violence, low-cost housing incentives, free transportation for relocation, and job opportunities in steel mills, railroads, meatpacking, and the auto industry drove millions of Black workers from their southern homes to the industrialized north. This rapid population growth resulted in large-scale housing shortages in northern cities (Rothstein 2017). Subsequently, the federal government implemented public housing for workers that was officially and explicitly segregated by race. These early housing laws laid the groundwork for what would become the segregation of American communities based overwhelmingly on race.

In chapter 4, we explain how racial-residential segregation continues to be a major factor in the perpetuation of Black-White inequality in the United States. Massey and Denton (1993) argue that sociologists have failed to fully consider racial-residential segregation as a leading factor in the construction of the Black ghetto, demonstrating both the intentional practices of individuals and institutions, as well as the actions in the private sector to construct and maintain racial segregation.

In chapter 5, we discuss how public schools in the United States continue to privilege Whiteness and White children at the expense of Black children. American public schools are largely staffed by White women who are not trained in culturally responsive pedagogy sensitive to the culture or needs of Black children, and who thus perpetuate the continuation of White, European curricula and the erasure of Black experiences and Black history. Moreover, due to neighborhood segregation, public schools remain segregated despite the *Brown v. Board of Education* ruling of 1954. Therefore, children in segregated Black communities continue to receive subpar education, attend schools that receive inadequate funding, experience higher teacher turnover rates, and employ School Resource Officers (SROs) who have deficit and often criminalized views of children of color. Not only this, but fueling the rapid incarceration of Black men is, in part, the school-to-prison pipeline—an industry powered by Black and Brown youth's early interaction with the juvenile justice system. When Black children are policed in their public schools, a culture of policing Black people grows in their communities. Early interaction with the juvenile justice system, including youth often being tried as adults, directly affects later opportunities and often further deters social mobility.

Chapters 6 and 7 concern the policing of both the literal and iconic ghetto. These chapters foreground Elijah Anderson's article "The Iconic Ghetto" (2012)—and scrutinize the ways in which Black people are perceived and policed regardless of their actual residential location or social status. We explore how the pervasive iconic nature of the ghetto affects the daily lives of Black people, informs policies implemented by our government and private industries, and fuels informal measures taken by White folks to ensure their status in the racial hierarchy.

In chapter 6, we demonstrate how the characterizations of Blackness fuel the rhetoric around how Black people are policed. Early depictions of Black men as criminals fueled the development of racist policies within the U.S. legal system and brought about the establishment of the War on Drugs. These policies, along with the hypersegregation of Black people in poor, isolated ghettos, have detrimental effects on Black people living in poor communities as well as those living outside them.

In chapter 7, we situate the contemporary police state in its historical context—how the U.S. penal system went from a once rehabilitative system to one based solely on punitive policies based on militarization, excessive force, and the over-policing of Black and Brown communities. Hirschfield (2015) finds that about six hundred thousand police officers patrol the streets of American cities every day and that, on average, two or three of them end up killing someone—meaning we have *daily* police killings in the United States. Moreover, Langton and Durose (2013) found that in 2011, over a hundred and fifty thousand Americans reported the use of "excessive force" during their most recent traffic stop. And despite early commitments to the "castle doctrine"—the idea that a person's home is their castle and homeowners should be protected from unnecessary violence—SWAT teams violently enter American homes more than one hundred times a day (Balko 2014).

The final chapter of the book, "Black Liberation, the Abolition Movement, and Where We Go from Here" covers the context in which the Black Lives Matter movement came to fruition, activist responses to policing from reform to abolition, and policy changes as they relate to educational inequality. This chapter provides the reader with some suggestions on how the U.S. might, as a nation, move from punitive policing toward a society in which communities are able to thrive, and where resources divert from policing and are funneled into mental health, schooling, jobs, and infrastructure. Moreover, this chapter covers the growing push to overhaul our existing education system to be more specifically antiracist to create an environment in which children can learn without fear of being criminalized.

CHAPTER 1

Slavery and the Social Construction of Race

> But in the same way that individuals cannot move forward, become whole and healthy, unless they examine the domestic violence they witnessed as children or the alcoholism that runs in their family, the country cannot become whole until it confronts what was not a chapter in its history, but the basis of its economic and social order. For a quarter millennium, slavery *was* the country.
>
> —Isabel Wilkerson

The impact of racialized systems in the contemporary United States on the daily lives of Black people is often spoken of as individual events—when "bad apples" stand apart from "most" Americans, as individual racists defying cultural norms of "color blindness." However, racial discrimination in American communities, streets, and schools is not a display of individual racism, but rather an extension of a culture of White supremacy—of people enacting the internalized system of racial oppression created by White people during colonialism and the transatlantic slave trade. Individual acts of racism are connected to a much more intricate and intentional system of racism, created to justify the supremacy of White landowners throughout the slavery era and to rationalize the brutal treatment of Native Americans during colonialism. While White supremacy may take different forms in contemporary America, it was born out of the ideologies that pervaded the thinking of American Whites during the 16th, 17th, and 18th centuries.

The Social Construction of Race

The world has not always been racialized—as in, the color of one's skin has not always carried with it a connotation of what privileges one is, or is not, entitled to. Nor has one's skin color always informed social expectations or assumptions about personality and character. The idea of race emerged out of a particular historical era under a specific set of social and political circumstances, including colonialism, the transatlantic slave trade, and the emergence of the plantation system (Allen 1994). Africans were not exploited and enslaved because they were Black. The transatlantic slave trade itself helped to create the very idea of Blackness and gave rise to the White/Black binary. Before this racialized view of the world, the major divisions between settler social groups in what became the United States were rooted in religion, even the subjugation and justification for the treatment of Native Americans was rooted in the belief that Christians were morally superior. Beliefs about superiority and inferiority around race did not develop until almost a hundred years into the slave trade. The myth of race developed not only to justify slavery but also to perpetuate the ideal of White superiority (Fitzgerald, in Meyerhoffer 2021) .

The racialization of the world began with European colonizers' early interactions with Native Americans. Natives' "way" of life disrupted European understandings of how human beings lived—thus, leading Europeans to question the extent to which Natives could be considered fully human and to consider the degree to which exploitation and enslavement of Natives could be justified. The forced labor of Natives, along with the enslavement of Africans throughout the African slave trade, birthed the racialization of people in the United States, beginning the early establishment of divisions between "Whites" and "others." The conquest of Native Americans was the first, and, arguably, the most important event in establishing a global racial awareness.

Specific policies established during the 16th and 17th centuries were intentionally designed to institute the United States as a White nation. For example, the Immigration Act of 1790 restricted citizenship to "any alien, being a free white person" who had been in the United States for at least two years. This effectively excluded indentured servants, the enslaved, and most women. This law simultaneously implied that Blacks and, later, Asians were ineligible for naturalization. Without the right to naturalize, one could not vote or yield political power—thus, giving White men a marked political advantage for decades to come. Herein, political and social power were exclusively controlled by White Americans responsible for creating and enforcing laws and policies that ultimately aimed to solely benefit White America and, inevitably, suppress the political and social advancement of Black people. Dually important was the Dred Scott decision of 1857, which, ultimately, established that no Black person, free or enslaved, could claim U.S. citizenship. The culmination of these events and sociopolitical decisions is that the history of the United States and its culture is, undoubtedly, grounded in and reproduced by Whiteness and White supremacy at large. White hegemony informed policies that both perpetuated and reinforced a racially divided nation (Martinot 2010).

While most social scientists recognize the social construction of race and its role in perpetuating white hegemony, biological definitions of race pervade the thinking of most Americans and perpetuate the weaponization of race as well as the continued notion that race is "real." Certainly, race is "real" in its consequences as it affects every aspect of American life; however, race is not "real" in the sense that human beings are biologically and inherently distinct from one another. While most social scientists and academics alike support the notion that race is a product of social expectations and creations, American culture reifies race as a social and structural reality that continues to yield debilitating outcomes for Black people. To better understand race, it is important that we recognize the origins of race as well as the social power it yields. Race remains one of the most powerful forces in defining people in the United States, so powerful that the very ideals of race and racial hierarchy incentivize racialized White groups and organizations to reinforce racial division and, oftentimes, forcefully exclude non-Whites from attaining social and political power—a most notable example being the Ku Klux Klan (Martinot 2010). Race indisputably signifies and symbolizes social conflict and human hierarchy (Meyerhoffer 2021).

There are a number of micro and macro factors that shaped and continue to shape racial categorization. The theory of racial formation is premised on the idea that racial projects pervade all aspects of society. Omi and Winant (1994) describe the ways in which society defers to race as means of "making up" and "othering" people. We use race to socially navigate our world, despite that race actually tells us very little about any given person. Racialization is the process through which we use physical aspects of a human body to denote social meaning, and we do this in a number of ways. How we *do* race and how we notice race within a system is what Omi and Winant call "racial projects." Authors Omi and Winant (1994, 21) assert, "Every racial project is both a reflection of and response to the broader patterning of race in the overall social system. In turn, every racial project attempts to reproduce, extend, subvert, or directly challenge that system." These projects take place at both macro and micro levels. Restrictive voting laws, stop-and-frisk laws, and lending policies through banks are examples of large-scale racial projects. The clothing one wears, locking car doors in a community perceived as being dangerous, a White family moving out of a neighborhood perceived as having too many people of color are examples of racial projects that occur at the small-scale level. In this vein, perceived essentialized differences in hair texture, skin color, physical stature, nose shape, and the like become connotations for social meanings such as intelligence, athletic ability, sexuality, temperament, and inclination toward criminal behavior. Once these physical characteristics become widely accepted as being related to social characteristics, the physical differences are no longer necessary to connote social meaning. These early racial differences, ultimately, became the rationale for contemporary discriminatory policies such as the disproportionate policing of Black communities, naturalization rights, residential segregation, and the mass incarceration of Black people.

The U.S. Racial Hierarchy

To understand contemporary racial inequality, it is pertinent that we, first, understand how a racial hierarchy emerged in the first place (Fitzgerald 2017). Slavery did not happen *because* of race or racism. Rather, race emerged as justification for the treatment of enslaved Africans and Native Americans in a "new world," presumed to be forming around values of freedom for everyone. During the slavery era, the United States was facing a moral conundrum of simultaneously upholding an inhumane institution while priding itself on democratic principles. As previously acknowledged, these democratic principles were not extended to all of its people. Because massive economic gains could be made by the enslavement and exploitation of Black labor in a growing capitalist system, Americans desperately sought a way to justify a gravely inhumane system of exploiting human labor.

It is important to acknowledge for historical context that Africans were not, in fact, the first choice for enslavement. European indentured servitude had already existed for incoming European immigrants, so this seemed a natural choice. However, White Europeans blended in more easily with the larger White population, which proved troublesome for slaveholders if they were to escape. European immigrants were also largely Christian, which complicated justification for enslavement on religious grounds. The enslavement of Native Americans was also practiced, but it was ultimately abandoned in most states as Natives either got sick and died or escaped and rejoined their tribes with the help of extensive knowledge of the region and the terrain. During the latter part of the 17th century, it became clear to slaveholders that Irish and Native Americans did not make ideal slaves, which led to a preference for enslaved Africans in American slavery as they were relatively inexpensive and not of Christian faith. As non-Christians, enslaved Africans were perceived as not fully human, which made enslaving them seem more justifiable. Enslaved Africans were considered less capable of successfully escaping and were less likely to effectively blend in with the larger White population. Ultimately, slavery became associated with Blackness and wage labor became associated with Whiteness.

Until the 18th century, Whites' opinion of Africans in socioeconomic terms was generally positive. They were considered superior laborers, perceived to have immunity to Old World diseases, and had nowhere to escape to in contrast to their European and Native counterparts. The colonists came to believe that they could not survive without Africans. This belief developed at the same time as so-called New World ideologies about freedom, equality, and liberty were widespread. Those involved in slave trade clung to the White hegemonic rationale that their actions were justifiable on the premise that Africans were heathens and it was their responsibility to save their souls. This rationale became a tool for slave traders and, in turn, allowed for the dissociation of seemingly contradictory emotions, such as guilt or shame, that may otherwise deter the progress of slavery.

Out of a need to justify slavery in the face of an antislavery movement in Europe and the United States, race evolved as an idea or set of ideas during the 18th century in America—originally rather ambiguously to denote a "kind" or "type" of person, but which ultimately divided Europeans, Native Americans, and Africans by the end of the 18th century. By combining physical attributes with social status, a new social identity was formed—one of race. One that attributes skin color to a host of social, emotional, and cognitive differences. Proslavery Americans fashioned a new identity, collapsing all European identities into one—White. This gave rise to the idea that race was biological and all the social, spiritual, moral, intellectual, and physical traits that go along with one's race are natural, innate, and immutable. Thus, U.S. slavery became the only slavery system in the world that was created and maintained solely on the basis of "race." By limiting a lifetime of servitude to Africans and their descendants, colonists were proclaiming that Blacks would forever remain at the bottom of the social hierarchy and, consequently, marginalized for decades to come. These same ideologies of inferiority were placed on both enslaved and free Blacks (Smedley 1999).

Whiteness as Normative/Becoming White

Early designations of "White" and "Black" were first used on ships during the Middle Passage. The crew wanted to distinguish themselves from their captives and referred to the cargo as "Black" and the crew as "White." It was through the slave trade during the 15th and 16th centuries that Europeans first began using racialized terms, which eventually became widespread among Americans as well.

Whiteness is not immutable, and those currently considered White in America were not always characterized so. Whiteness is something that "came to be" and continues to evolve based on the given political and cultural climate (Jacobson 1998). For example, Irish immigrants were perceived as inferior upon arrival to the United States, but they prioritized assimilation as means of dissociating themselves from their fellow "non-Whites" at the time. For example, Irish immigrants were not considered part of the Anglo-Saxon majority until they clearly and deliberately distanced themselves as separate from free and enslaved Black people. Due to direct competition for jobs, space, and political power, Irish immigrants saw Black people as threatening rather than as working-class allies (Roediger 1999). Rather than forming alliances with other "races," they distanced themselves from Black and Brown communities in attempt to align themselves with the White communities. Through a long process of assimilation, the Irish came to be considered and accepted as White by moving toward the dominant group and away from other racial groups, and intentionally so.

Whiteness is observed to have been created over three different historical periods. Jacobson (1998) establishes three great epochs of Whiteness: the first from 1790–1840; the second from the 1840s–1920s; and the third from the 1920s through the present. These three epochs established not only who "counts" as White but also how we perceive Whiteness, and who has the power to decide which members fit into a given racial category. Beginning during early colonization and continuing through the mid-19th century, only "free White" immigrants were considered citizens—this included Anglo-Saxons and northern Europeans. From the mid-19th century through the early 20th century, immigrants from southern, central, and eastern Europe began challenging the boundaries of Whiteness to shed their "other" status. Originally these groups were considered inferior, and their later acceptance as White required a broadening of the definition of Whiteness. The White/Black binary, downplaying ethnic differences among Whites, has only been considered prominent since the 1920s. Out of this binary, a more generic White identity was formed.

Eugenics, Scientific Racism, and Phrenology

Scientific racism is the process of employing scientific methods in an attempt to prove innate racial inferiority among some groups and superiority among others. Scientific racism arose in response to the question of the morality of slavery. Scientists used various "scientific" methods to prove that the enslavement of Black people was not morally inhumane based on the premise that Blacks were not fully human. Scientific racism became a powerful tool in justifying a racially informed social order. One of the earliest examples of scientific racism is the study of phrenology—a branch of science that compared the skull sizes of different racial groups to determine intelligence levels and various other social and cultural characteristics. Phrenologists would use skulls to demonstrate objective, innate differences between races. Scientists would measure facial angles, hair texture, bone structure, and other physical attributes to demonstrate the innate biological differences between racial groups. In support of these practices and efforts, several scientific journals went on to publish these results, further legitimizing claims that race was biological (Fitzgerald 2017). Herein, the realm of science, which was and still is predominately White, served to reinforce racialized ideals of hierarchal stratification that posits Blacks as inferior to Whites; moreover, these racialized beliefs were confirmed as fact and, therefore, considered indisputable—ideologies that still pervade the ways in which race affects the lives of Americans today.

Throughout the age of Enlightenment, the theory of polygenesis—the idea that races are separate species—was the subject of intellectual and religious debate (Kendi 2019). This debate peaked during the 1770s in response to the transatlantic antislavery movement. Despite President Jefferson's support for monogenesis, polygenesis dominated racial thought throughout the United States. This hegemonic ideology influenced and informed policies aimed at re-enslaving or killing those perceived to be genetically inferior. While polygenesis was a highly contested theory in academia, it pervaded common thought throughout the United States for at least four hundred years.

The emergence of scientific racism, ultimately, gave rise to the eugenics movement—a movement rooted in the notion that the healthiest and most able-bodied should be encouraged to reproduce for the betterment of society. This movement gave rise to anti-miscegenation laws, involuntary sterilizations, and republican motherhood—the last a term referring to White women's contribution to "growing the republic" (Fitzgerald 2017). Scientific racism was based on the idea that superior races produced superior cultures, whereas inferior races produced inferior cultures. In this regard, "Whites" were encouraged to reproduce for the betterment of humankind, while other racial groups were discouraged from reproducing and commonly subjected to involuntary sterilizations. Social Darwinism and the eugenics movement gave rise to anti-miscegenation laws, which forbade interracial marriage, relationships, and sex based on the idea that the White race needed to remain "pure" and free of inferior contamination through cross-race reproduction.

Despite a growing understanding that there is, ultimately, no such thing as racial ancestry—that, genetically, human beings are 99.9 percent the same (Fitzgerald 2014)—the perpetuation of the racial purity ideology and the belief that race is, somehow, genetically driven continues to pervade all aspects of American life today. Race plays a role in shaping where people live, the jobs they have access to, the schools they go to, and how they are treated by the criminal justice system. Race may not be scientifically genetic, but it is most certainly real and continues to function as one of the most influential determining factors of one's life in the United States. The end of slavery as we know it did not, in fact, bring an end to racist ideologies. While slavery has formally ended from a legal standpoint, nothing was done, or has been done, to dismantle the racial hierarchy and racist ideologies that were born out of this era (Stevenson 2017). Because White identity was and is grounded in and formed around the belief of superiority, Whites resisted notions of equality among newly "freed" Blacks and, instead, created new systems to uphold the same racist ideals. These systems remain in place today and continue to manifest themselves in our neighborhoods, schools, and criminal justice system.

Racialization, Neighborhoods, and Policing

The racial classification system that was birthed during slavery and exacerbated during the eugenics movement continues to affect Black people and inform American culture, even now—157 years after slavery ended. For example, housing policy in the United States was established along racially explicit lines with the specific goal of keeping White and Black residents in racially homogenous communities and limiting Blacks' access to White neighborhoods—policies that we continue to see the effects of today. Additionally, the system of policing within the United States was created to protect the "property" of middle-income Whites—property at the time included enslaved people. Early slave patrols were created to round up, brutalize, and terrorize runaway slaves. These patrols, while initially informal, led to the establishment of a formal system of policing composed of policies aimed at controlling Black people—both free and enslaved. The exact mechanisms within American housing and policing that were used to control and limit the opportunities of Black people are addressed in later chapters, but it is important to understand that early systems of racialization and racial hierarchy are what created the foundations on which modern racism is based. Moreover, these exclusionary systems of oppression laid the foundation for how Black people are treated within our public education system—leaving them with little access to quality education, the experience of punitive policing from an early age, and being regularly targeted by teachers, staff, and school resource officers.

CHAPTER 2

Slave Patrols and Early Law Enforcement

> The first real organized policing systems in America arguably began in the South with slave patrols. The patrols were armed and uniformed, and typically had broad powers to arrest, search, and detain slaves.
>
> —Radley Balko

The creation of modern American policing has a multitude of roots, but it is most significantly tied to the institution of slavery and the themes of residual socioeconomic control. Studies show that White fear of slave rebellions helped to fuel the development of strict laws to control the lives and mobility of Black people. The history of policing in the South is linked to White patrollers' preoccupation with the daily proceedings and activities of enslaved Blacks (Hadden 2003). Fugitive slave laws, dating from 1793 to 1850, were enacted to allow the "detention and return of escaped slaves." These laws incentivized control-efforts with compensation for returned slaves and were primarily upheld by slave patrols and slave hunters, along with their dogs of which they referred to as "packs of Negro dogs" (Rawick 1972; Spruill 2016, 52). Slave patrols and night watches—both of which laid the foundations for modern police departments—were created to control and regulate the behaviors and lives of Black and Native populations. The need to impose strict supervisions upon the lives of Black people eventually led to the formal formation of local police departments whose sole responsibility was to protect the interests of White middle-class citizens, which, ultimately, served to uphold White supremacy and ensure Black subordination.

Slave Patrols

Posse comitatus were bands of men in early modern England tasked with locating and arresting fleeing felons, which served as an early model for slave patrolling in the New World (Hadden 2003). The first slave patrol was created in Carolina in 1704, and by the time John Adams became president in 1797, every state that had yet to abolish slavery, including northern states, had slave patrols. The control of labor largely fueled the rationalization of patrollers, as it was considered essential to the successful rise of industrialization and capitalism. Out of a need to control the labor force for the production of cotton, rice, and tobacco, White property owners created and enforced a system of racially explicit laws designed to strike terror into the entire Black community. Slave patrols were typically composed of three to six White men armed with guns, ropes, and whips that would be used to terrorize and apprehend any Black person perceived to be escaping or plotting a revolt. Somewhat surprisingly, slave patrols included Whites of all social classes as it was considered the collective responsibility of the White community to protect itself from any perceived threats of violence, crime, and rebellion (Spruill 2016; Hadden 2003). While the main concern of slave patrols was the management of enslaved Blacks, they also supervised suspicious Whites and free Blacks who were believed to fraternize with those who were enslaved. A number of infractions could warrant a beating from patrollers, including attending weddings, funerals or church services, mingling with Whites, "back talk," dressing tidily, and singing songs and hymns (Fountain 2018; Hadden 2003). These White patrollers were known for extreme cruelty, armed on both foot and horseback and often accompanied by bloodhounds. The use of bloodhounds specifically to hunt fugitive slaves operationalized the dehumanizing rhetoric that surrounded Blackness in the South (Spruill 2016). Use of canine violence is contrary to the sacredness of humanity—signaling the prevailing notions of Black inferiority. Slave patrols were designed to terrorize and punish the enslaved population while assisting wealthy landowners to control people who were considered mere property. Slave patrollers were emboldened to enter the home of anyone, regardless of race or ethnicity, if they were suspected to be harboring enslaved people. The role of slave patrols was not only to return fugitive slaves, but to also police and control the movement of all Black people, including free Blacks (Barlow and Barlow 1999). Free Blacks who did not have proper documentation on them at all times could be sold to southern slaveholders and, thus, have their identity as "free" revoked (Jackson 2009; Hadden 2003). Not even freedom papers—documents that free Blacks carried to prove their liberated status from slavery—exempted free Blacks from imprisonment, violent harassment, or being sold into slavery (Jackson 2009; Hadden 2003, 114–15). The liberty extended to slave patrols leveraged them with a tremendous amount of power that only further perpetuated White supremacist ideologies that placed Blacks as wholly inferior and inhuman.

PATROLS IN THE SOUTH

The earliest slave patrol system in the United States dates back to 1704, a structure originally developed in Barbados and imported into South Carolina, with most other southern slaveholding colonies and states soon following suit. As a means of ensuring economic prosperity, Black labor was deemed essential to southern progressive efforts and yet also paradoxically considered threatening to White people. White southerners' desire to preserve power over the enslaved was in response to collective White fear of slave rebellion and, perhaps most prominently, served to preserve the core ideology of White supremacy (Spruill 2016, 50; Hadden 2003, 6). Toward the end of the 17th century in South Carolina and throughout the mid-18th century in both Virginia and North Carolina, legislatures established colony-sanctioned authority figures tasked with monitoring slave movement (Jackson 2009, 169). Patrols were grouped primarily with respect to the lay of the land, especially in terms of rivers, swamps, and creeks. These divided territories would later become county lines. Slave patrols, or "paddy rollers" as they were commonly referred to, led to the first publicly funded police departments in the American South and served to both manage race-based conflict and control enslaved populations (Walker 1980, in Durr 2015; Fountain 2018).

Slave patrollers were granted near limitless power to act with brute force and employed bloodhounds, whips, and guns as means of controlling Black people so as to maintain White dominance. These patrollers moved fairly freely across plantation grounds and were allowed to enter slave quarters as desired to incite beatings in the event that captives were storing books, paper, weapons, liquor, or any other presumed luxuries (Fountain 2018). Gatherings of any sort on behalf of Black people was viewed as a threat, including weddings and funerals, and often resulted in beatings (Hadden 2003; Walker 1980, in Durr 2015).

PATROLS IN THE NORTH

Slavery was not confined to southern states as many would believe, though there tends to be more documentation regarding slave patrolling in that region. Slavery in the north during the 18th century looked significantly different than in the South. Enslaved people in New England were a small minority in contrast to those in southern states, constituting roughly 2 to 3 percent of the population, and they were concentrated in the coastal urban areas and along rivers and estuaries.

Although mid-Atlantic colonies had larger populations, enslaved people were geographically positioned in the same ways. Slaveholders in the New England area ranged from wealthy gentlemen to shopkeepers and artisans (White 2003, 18). Slavery was not a definitive way of life, so much as a response to immediate labor needs; slaveholders were far more flexible in allowing those who were enslaved to work and sleep alongside them. Moreover, there was a notably higher turnover rate of slaves from one owner to the next in the North. The apparently looser, smaller-scale nature of northern slavery was a presumed aspect of tempering the brutality of the system. Nevertheless, New York, Connecticut, and other colonies upheld fugitive slave laws that worked to criminalize and control enslaved people from 1793 to 1850. Northeastern colonies developed and came to rely on an informal night-watch system, predominantly made up of volunteers tasked with ensuring the security of properties (Fountain 2018). Night-watch groups in the north were accompanied by sheriffs and other authority figures, whose shared tasks were to maintain order, control the enslaved, and regulate civic engagement. Whereas slave patrols of the South roamed assigned territories specifically to control the movement of enslaved people, the role of night watchmen in the north was not as specific but aided in those efforts.

Reconstruction

The 13th Amendment to the U.S. Constitution was passed on December 6, 1865. It prohibited slavery throughout the United States "except as punishment for crime." Herein, "except for punishment for crime" served as somewhat of a clause by which an alternative avenue for the continuation of slavery presented itself within the confines of constitutional language. During Reconstruction, law enforcement could no longer be explicitly racialized. While slave patrolling ceased to operate upon the close of the Civil War, its functions remained very much intact through the agency of other organizations and institutions (Hadden 2003). While law enforcement activities consisted of checking in on suspicious activities, the extrajudicial activities were carried out by vigilante groups whose tactics closely mirrored that of slave patrols. It is necessary to note that slavery itself also did not end after the Civil War and conditions for newly freed Blacks were, arguably, worse due to the rise in vigilante violence. The absence of the formal system of slavery left Black people vulnerable to increasingly heinous acts of violence as their economic value declined within the system of White capitalism (Fountain 2018).

Racist and prevailing ideologies of Black people as subhuman encouraged the growth of vigilante groups and lynch mobs without threat of external restraints during Reconstruction. Federal military personnel, members of the Ku Klux Klan

(KKK), and state militia emerged from disbanded slave patrols with the common goal of upholding White supremacy and controlling the newly freed Black population. These groups were known to be much harsher than their predecessors. Ultimately, these extrajudicial groups began to operate like the newly established police departments in the United States (Durr 2015). The most infamous vigilante group, the KKK, was formed in the 1860s and was known for lynching, whipping, and other egregious acts of violence against Blacks. The KKK was skillful in organizing and aimed to elicit the maximum amount of fear, so much so that the appearance of their white-hooded attire and flaming torches drove deep fear into Black communities. The KKK often gathered, patrolled, and terrorized Black communities during the night. White southerners revered the KKK as true law enforcement and condoned their unrestrained conduct toward Black people in the name of preserving White dominance (Spruill 2016, 59). It was common practice for law enforcement officers to also be members of the KKK (Hadden 2003). The lynching of Black people was not constrained to the South, but happened in colonies across the nation. In 1871, the Ku Klux Klan Act was passed and served to prohibit any state official from participating in any act that violated the civil rights of any citizen. This was due, in large part, to the involvement of law enforcement officials in vigilante groups, namely the KKK. Unsurprisingly, this legislation yielded little impact as White supremacist groups continued to populate police forces well into the 1960s. The use of patrols to terrorize Black communities persisted long after the Civil Rights Act of 1964 and remains an element of policing in contemporary police forces today (Turner, Giacopassi, and Vandiver 2006). The following four factors are commonly associated with the early organizing of police forces: actual or perceived increase in crime, public insurrections or riots, public intoxication, and the perceived need to control "dangerous classes" (Spruill 2016, 49–50). These factors are deeply connected to the formation of slave patrolling.

The exact transition from slave patrols to formal policing in the United States continues to be contested by scholars—some asserting that slave patrols were the first formal attempt at policing in the United States, while others argue that while policing was born out of slave patrols, organized formal policing did not come until later. Slave patrols formally dissolved at the end of the Civil War, but formerly enslaved people were quickly subject to Black codes. Black codes were, originally, designed to provide Black people equal protection under federal law, though the 14th Amendment delegitimatized them (Jackson 2009, 172). Yet, in the end, they dictated where Black people were allowed to work, travel, and live; they also dictated how much they were paid and restricted voting rights. Black codes presumably granted Blacks freedom, but they assigned such extensive restrictions that they increasingly infringed on the freedoms of Black people. The North perceived the implementation of Black codes as an attempt by the South to defy the North by way of re-enslaving Black people in accordance with their long-standing opposing views (Browning 1930, 471–72). Black codes were made illegal in 1868, but were followed by decades of Jim Crow laws (1870s–1960s), designed to deny Black people their civil rights. Jim Crow laws upheld White supremacy by enforcing the segregation of public space for Black and White Americans—maintaining separate schools, libraries, water fountains, restaurants, and more. Blacks who broke these laws were subject to police brutality and other acts of cruelty, both physical and psychological. Vigilante groups were rarely punished for lynching Black people or for enacting extrajudicial killings. Blacks were regularly subject to police violence for violating laws aimed at controlling the Black population. The overt negligence of the justice system to hold police accountable for failing to protect the lives of Black people continues to this day.

Slave Patrols and Modern Policing

Upon closer examination of slave patrolling and night-watch groups within the United States, their foundational role in the creation of a more formal, racially focused law enforcement becomes unavoidably evident (Hadden 2003). Modern-day police practices are not far removed from the slave patrols in the South, night watches, or the vigilante groups that remain today. To this end, Sally Hadden asserts that "most early law enforcement, by definition, consisted of White patrolmen watching, catching, or beating Black slaves" (2003, 4). Several other scholars agree and assert that slave patrols were a precursor to contemporary policing patterns and that in all states, armed slave patrols would scour the land looking to control and terrorize the Black population (e.g., Spruill 2016). The similarities between modern policing and the system of slave patrols are far too striking to continue to ignore. Slave patrols are, justifiably, considered the foundation of contemporary law enforcement in the United States (Turner, Giacopassi, and Vandiver 2006, 186). While conceptions of policing essentially center the maintenance of social order, the other, less known, function of law enforcement is to enforce the racial hierarchy.

Remnants of these racialized systems of policing remain intact as certain elements of policing in the contemporary United States are clearly tied to early systems of policing. While Black people no longer need passes to demonstrate their status as "free," they continue to be overpoliced, racially profiled, and disproportionately subject to police brutality and fatality. Policies such as "stop and frisk" echo the historical tradition of stopping Black people for merely existing, often for being in "White spaces" and failing to show deference to White people or for appearing in stereotypically perceived suspicious or "criminal" ways (Anderson 2011). Similarly, nightly curfews and vagrancy laws are derived from the patrolling era and are continuously reinforced, particularly in response to protesting police brutality and the wrongful deaths of Black people (Hadden 2003, 59). While these connections seem abundantly apparent, the link between patrolling and contemporary police enforcement go, overwhelmingly, unacknowledged. Refusal to acknowledge the link between slavery and contemporary law enforcement is to ignore the blatant and obvious roots of racism within American policing. David Embrick points out that several scholars (Michael Omi, Howard Winant, Eduardo Bonilla-Silva, Joe Feagin, and Michelle Alexander) analogize modern-day policing as "old perfume repackaged in a new bottle" (Embrick 2015). Procedural protection for police officers after they shoot civilians is not that dissimilar to that of slave patrollers' after conducting similar acts of violence. Racial and ethnic violence in the name of law enforcement persists to this day, and it is not difficult to see the remnants of early slave patrols in contemporary policing, particularly in predominantly Black communities. Groups, beginning with slave patrols, kept White supremacy intact for decades to come and now assume the form of law enforcement.

Policing Black Communities

The freedom with which contemporary police forces are provided power to terrorize, control, and overpolice Black communities throughout the nation speaks volumes about a system that upholds White supremacy in both overt and covert ways. The connections between slavery, the Jim Crow era, and policing practices are, arguably, undeniable. One of the many examples we may pull from is the U.S. Department of Justice's investigation into the lethal killing of Michael Brown in Ferguson, Missouri. Results, released on March 4, 2015, conclude that the Ferguson police force routinely violated the constitutional rights of residents by disproportionately targeting Black people and applying racial stereotypes to Black residents in a racially discriminatory manner (U.S. Department of Justice 2015, 4). This DOJ report exposes decades of racist policing, corruption, and excessive use of police force. The Ferguson Police Department was also found guilty of unjustly deploying the excessive use of police dogs to terrorize and torture Black people, further infringing upon constitutional rights (Spruill 2016, 44–45). The practice of employing canine units in police departments is derived directly from slave patrolling tactics and, ultimately, works to achieve the same goal of perpetuating racial oppression. While the use of canines has been abandoned by some police units, recent reports (e.g., U.S. Department of Justice 2015) indicate that the Ferguson Police Department still uses this tactic primarily to target Black offenders—a violation of their constitutional rights. The severity of police departments' employment of canine units is grossly overlooked due to the erasure of its historical bond to the use of bloodhounds by patrollers (Spruill 2016).

Contemporary policing enforced within Black communities has not changed in any inherent way by comparison to the policing of enslaved people and, later, freed Blacks during Reconstruction. While policies may be less explicitly racialized in language, the effects remain the same. Realities such as stop and frisk, racial profiling, or "driving while black" are all remnants of the same system designed to control, contain, and terrorize Black people. In Black communities, police encounters are more likely to result in arrest and involve the use of coercive force; traffic stops are more likely to lead to searches and citations (Drakulich and Crutchfield 2013, 387). Michael Brown was one of four unarmed Black men killed by the Ferguson, Missouri, police department in a single month (Lee 2014). The DOJ's Police Public Contact Survey of 2008 finds that Black people surpass their White and Hispanic counterparts in being most likely to experience threat or use of force by police officers (cited in Lee 2014). In 2015, police killed at least 104 unarmed Black people, accounting for 36 percent of unarmed people killed by police despite constituting only 13 percent of the U.S. population—a rate that is five times higher than the rate of unarmed Whites being killed by police in 2015 (mappingpoliceviolence.org).

Perhaps most importantly, rates of crime do not correlate with rates of police killings. For example, in cities such as Buffalo and Newark, crime rates are relatively high but with relatively low rates of police violence. Conversely, Spokane and Orlando have relatively low crime rates but high rates of police violence. Thus, police killings of unarmed Black people are much more likely related to perceptions of Blackness rather than actual crime rates. Gaping inequities are found in police conduct, in which Black people are more likely to experience police violence, regardless of the presence of criminal activity or not, as compared with their White counterparts (Kramer et al. 2017, 23). Kramer and others convey that race is a leading factor in whether one may be the victim of police violence over a host of other circumstances, including time of day, subject's height, age, gender, and behavior (2017, 23). Spruill (2016) appropriately quotes an excerpt from George W. Carleton's *Suppressed Book about Slavery* (1864) in arguing that

> Slavery is not dead yet. It is pretending to be dead, only that it may be let alone and rise again to do mischief. It has had hard knocks, and is half dead. It would be

> madness not to kill the surviving half. We want peace, but not peace that will last only till our children shall grow up to partake of a legacy of blood and an inheritance of curses. (59–60)

Written in 1864, these words still ring true nearly 150 years later with respect to the institutionalization of racism for which contemporary law enforcement was founded. It is no accident that Black people disproportionately face threats and violence (often fatal) at the hands of law enforcement; a contextual understanding of how the institution of policing was founded on overt racism helps us to see so.

Perceptions of Police and Race

With this context in mind, it is easier to understand why scholars continue to find that perceptions of police vary by race and that Blacks tend to hold more negative views of police than Whites. Race continues to be one of the most consistent predictors of attitudes toward police. A national survey conducted in 2002 finds that most Blacks and Hispanics believe that police in their respective cities treat both Blacks and Hispanics worse than Whites. In contrast, Whites do not agree with this view and are of the view that police treat Hispanics, Blacks, and Whites equally. This same study reveals that most Blacks and Hispanics find that the police offer worse service to those in Black and Hispanic neighborhoods; a statement that only one-third of Whites agree with. Perhaps most alarming is that Whites are less likely than Blacks and Hispanics to believe racial prejudice is a problem (Weitzer and Tuch 2005, 1017). To believe that racial prejudice is not a problem exacerbates racialized injustices at the hands of officers and law enforcement. Whites are more likely to perceive incidences of police discrimination as isolated, rather than systemically widespread). Nevertheless, these findings point to the notion that Black people are far more likely to hold negative views of the police in comparison to Whites (Weitzer and Steven 2005, 1010).

Perceptions of police injustice are closely related to individuals' race, as well as the overall racial composition of one's neighborhood. Racial differences in perceptions of the police are shaped by the increased likelihood of BIPOC (Black, Indigenous, and people of color) experiencing negative police-citizen encounters. Black people express a greater lack of faith in the criminal justice system, and justifiably so, and describe a disinterest on the part of law enforcement to address community problems. Low evaluations of the police are far more common in neighborhoods perceived as having higher levels of poverty, crime, and disorder. Black communities perceive police to yield less efficacy, which is shaped by the belief that police are biased toward Blacks and mistreat local residents (Drakulich and Crutchfield 2013, 394).

Policing, Neighborhoods, and Schools

The system of policing does not stand alone in its oppression and control of Black people but overlaps and intersects with housing and education in several ways. The American housing system, too, has an overtly racist history and is riddled with racially informed practices aimed at segregating and controlling the Black community. When policing is coupled with our housing system and its history of racial segregation, we see the overpolicing, occupation, and surveillance of Black neighborhoods most often by officers residing outside the community they are policing. Due to housing segregation, racial stereotyping, and limited interaction with the Black community, White police officers have deficit views of Black people individually and collectively. This increases the likelihood that excessive force is used during a confrontation—this is likely whether officers are in a Black neighborhood or not. Housing segregation, characterizations of Blackness and criminality, and the perpetuation of Black people as representing the "ghetto" result in officers being more likely to view Black people, particularly Black men, as dangerous, inclined to criminal activity, and threatening regardless of the context in which the interaction is taking place (Anderson 2012). Moreover, specific policies such as stop-and-frisk policing and a "zero-tolerance drug policy" disproportionately affect Black people residing in segregated Black neighborhoods. When policing is coupled with our public education system, we are more likely to see School Resource Officers (SROs) act with excessive force in schools that are predominately Black. Here, we see the early criminalization of Black children, increased suspension rates, and the rapid fueling of the school-to-prison pipeline—all issues that are addressed in greater detail in the chapters to come.

The systems of policing, housing, and education all oppress and marginalize Black people individually. Yet, when combined, the effects are catastrophic and serve to uphold and perpetuate White supremacy on a large-scale in an overlapping and unrelenting system of racial oppression.

CHAPTER 3

The Great Migration and Early Housing Segregation

> With segregation, with the isolation of the injured and the robbed, comes the concentration of disadvantage. An unsegregated America might see poverty, and all its effects, spread across the country with no particular bias toward skin color. Instead, the concentration of poverty has been paired with a concentration of melanin.
>
> —Ta-Nehisi Coates

Most people living in the United States can identify neighborhoods in their communities that are primarily populated by specific racial or ethnic groups, and they are able to verbally distinguish where racial and ethnic groups are concentrated within their communities. However, what most people are unable to do is identify *why* this is. The ideology that residential location is predominately influenced by individual choice is prominent among many Americans, presuming that racial groups generally live segregated from one another because it is their preference to "live with their own." This narrow perspective lacks historical and sociological understanding as to how American neighborhoods have been shaped not by personal choice but, rather, intentional government policy aimed at keeping Black people out of White neighborhoods. It is imperative to acknowledge that racialized, sociopolitical prejudice and discrimination are more determinant factors in Black-White segregation than any other presumed ethnocentric preference for same-race neighborhoods. In fact, African Americans, as well as Hispanics and Asians, are more inclined to express a residential preference for integrated neighborhoods in comparison to Whites (Iceland and Wilkes 2006, 250). Regardless of individual or group preference, institutional racism leads to the separation of racial groups, disinvestment in racially mixed or non-White communities, and the directing of investment and accompanying resources to homogenous all-White communities (Mendez et al. 2011, 103).

The ways in which our neighborhoods continue to be segregated is the result of a number of macro and micro factors, but the *creation* of segregated White communities is the result of racially explicit federal government policy, later reinforced at the state and local levels. Most scholars distinguish between de jure and de facto segregation with the former being the result of policies and practices that are legally recognized; an example of this being Jim Crow segregation in southern states. However, when looking at residential segregation in the Northeast and Midwest, scholars regularly refer to this as de facto segregation—segregation that is practiced but not legally recognized. Yet, any examination of government policy from Reconstruction until the last quarter of the 20th century quite clearly demonstrates that racial-residential segregation is the result of not only de facto practices but also deliberate and explicit de jure regulations designed to maintain the homogeneity of White neighborhoods (Massey 2015). Although de jure policies are no longer legally recognized, their effects have yet to be remedied and continue to negatively affect the living conditions and experiences of Black people within the United States. The persisting racial-residential segregation of Black communities further cements generational poverty and, thus, perpetuates a highly disadvantaged socioeconomic environment for Black families (Massey 2017, 800). To be clear, an intentional racial-caste system was created in this country that premeditatively excludes Black people from a number of resources and opportunities otherwise afforded to Whites, namely access to equitable housing and entrance into White neighborhoods (Massey 2015). Massey (2017, 800) contends that no other racial group in the history of the United States has been subject to the degree of separation that Black people experience and that the lasting effects of de jure segregation continue today through racialized behavior, institutional practices, and prejudicial public policies. Despite the disadvantages Black Americans faced after the Civil War, they were never as residentially segregated from Whites as they continue to be in the Northeast and the Midwest (Massey and Denton 1993, 17). Some of these hypersegregated metropolitan areas within the United States include Baltimore, Boston, Chicago, Cleveland, Detroit, Flint, Kansas City, Milwaukee, New York, Philadelphia, and St. Louis (Massey 2017, 800).

The Great Migration

Throughout the late 19th century and into the early 20th century, immigrants entered the United States at a consistent, steady pace and gravitated toward cities; cities served as the preferential location for integration, assimilation, and economic stability upon arrival into the United States. However, Black people experienced a very different process of residential settling upon the illegalization of slavery, as they were barred from many of the resources and opportunities otherwise accessible to immigrants. Urban environments and communities served to entrap Black people in the lower class for generations to come. Many high-occupancy buildings were constructed during this time, but they were primarily tailored to White factory workers. The areas where Black people were allowed to live were in areas deemed unconducive to further employment opportunities and upward social mobility (Massey and Denton 1993; Rothstein 2017).

The Great Migration of roughly six million Black people out of southern states and into northern industrialized urban spaces between 1910–70 was one of the most significant demographic shifts the nation has experienced to date. During World War I, African Americans began migrating to the North at a significant rate, far greater than the previous four decades had seen, and this continued well through World War II. World War I labor shortages in northern factories were attractive to southern Black people who had limited economic opportunities. The ill-fated promise of less race-related violence, low-cost housing incentives, free transportation for relocation, and job opportunities in steel mills, railroads, meatpacking, and the auto industry drove millions of Black workers to leave their southern homes and relocate to the industrialized north. By 1930, roughly one-quarter of thirty- to forty-year-old southern-born Black men resided outside the South (Collins and Wanamaker 2014, 221). Consequently, the Great Black Migration triggered a greater surge of prejudice and discrimination, giving rise to residential segregation through means of White-on-Black violence, in which Blacks seeking entry into White neighborhoods were met with White mobs, home bombings, shootings, and arson. Black "ghettos" were consequently cemented through a culmination of these earlier tactics and policies aimed at maintaining the racial divide (Massey 2015).

Although slavery became outlawed and invoked the promise of freedom for Black people, this hope was quickly falsified and stunted through a new form of legal racial marginalization known as the Jim Crow era. Black people were legally isolated from social areas inhabited by Whites under the conditions of Jim Crow laws (Williams and Collins 2001). Further fueling rapid migration was growing racism in the South, Jim Crow segregation, widespread lynching of Black people, and limited social and economic mobility within southern states (Tolnay 2003). The effects of slavery remained intact as White communities maintained power through the suppression of Black people; the economic, political, and social suffering of Blacks superseded the abolishment of slavery through the Jim Crow era (Asante 2008). Few studies consider racial-residential segregation to be an important causal factor of persisting poverty and socioeconomic marginalization within urban communities and the underclasses (Massey and Denton 1993). This is an oversight.

Government Policy and the Shaping of American Neighborhoods

It is not just one policy that is responsible for the segregation of American neighborhoods, but a series of policies and laws enacted by the American government. Federal, state, and local governments used public housing policy, redlining, blockbusting, as well as banking and lending regulations to purposely segregate every metropolitan area in the nation. These racialized practices lead to a significant, and apparent, difference of experiences in the home-searching process. For example, Blacks are less likely to use a real estate agent in comparison with Whites. Bearing in mind the findings of numerous studies conducted surrounding the implementation of racist practices in the real estate sector, it is of no surprise that Black people are more reluctant to use this service (Massey and Lundy 2001). Another extension of racial profiling in the real estate sector is linguistic profiling, whereby agents presume one's race and act with discrimination toward perceived non-Whites. Massey and Lundy find that African Americans, African American women in particular, face linguistic profiling in comparison to other non-White racial groups. In addition to blockbusting, real estate agents use a range of tactics to steer White families away from Black homes and vice versa when showing houses to prospective homeowners.

PUBLIC HOUSING THEN AND NOW

The rapid population growth during the Great Migration resulted in large-scale housing shortages in northern cities. Subsequently, the federal government implemented public housing for workers that was officially and explicitly segregated by race. The Kerner Commission of 1968 reported that the United States was divided into two distinct societies segregated by race, separate and unequal. In several cities across America, housing for White workers and Black workers were constructed in separate areas. In areas where public housing was shared, integrated activities were forbidden, and social programming and recreational activities had to be scheduled separately (Rothstein 2017).

Between 1933 and 1973 roughly one million public housing units were proposed and built. The federal public housing program began during the early 1930s in prolonged response to concerns regarding low-income housing conditions and residual slums. Slums were associated with higher rates of disease, crime, and delinquency. The first federally funded public housing units were developed between 1933 and 1937 under the New Deal. The Public Works Administration (PWA) was responsible for the construction of just over twenty-one thousand units across thirty-six metropolitan areas within the United States. The Housing Acts of 1937 and 1949 followed suit in expanding geographically and replaced the Housing Division of the PWA with the United States Housing Authority (USHA) in 1937 (Shester 2013, 981). Worth noting, the Housing Act of 1937 authorized an eligibility requirement contingent on residents' status as low-income in which tenants were not allowed to make more than four times local fair market rent; tenants that surpassed this threshold were evicted. The USHA's goals were communicated broadly as providing financial assistance, eliminating unsafe and unsanitary conditions, eradicating slums, and reducing unemployment rates in hopes of stimulating the economy. A total of a hundred and sixty thousand units were built under USHA between 1937 and 1949. The Housing Act of 1949 was similar to the Housing Act of 1937, with the exception of the "equivalent elimination." This required that with the construction of each new public housing development, any unsafe or unsanitary unit be either demolished or repaired. Toward the late 1950s, criticism of public housing emerged arguing that it institutionalized and exacerbated slums. Due to price ceilings on each unit, construction quality was subpar and resulted in the rapid deterioration of units (Shester 2013, 983).

While many Americans are likely to associate public housing with poor Black people, public housing was in fact originally created for low- to middle-class White families (Rothstein 2017). Black people were originally exempt from public housing and forced to live in overpopulated, dilapidated slums. Beginning during World War II and continuing through 1955, the purpose of public housing was not to house people who were unable to afford housing, but rather to house those unable to find housing due to the rapid population growth in industrialized cities. Roosevelt's New Deal created the nation's first public housing for civilians in response to the growing housing shortage, resulting from the Great Depression and World War II. Early public housing units were low-rise and maintained several disqualifying factors including irregular employment history, criminal records, out-of-wedlock birth, mental illness, and narcotic addiction. Early public housing either segregated Black people into separate buildings or excluded them entirely. Once projects were open to White and Black residents, they had to reflect the neighborhood racial composition. Black public housing units at the onset of the New Deal were very poorly maintained and fell below proper living conditions, most notably in Atlanta, Georgia (Ruechel 1997). Not surprisingly, deteriorating housing conditions pose health and safety concerns. The lasting effects of housing segregation by race continues to be maintained and exacerbated today.

BANKING AND LENDING

In an attempt to grow the economy during the 1930s and save working- and middle-class homeowners from defaulting on their loans, the Home Owners' Loan Corporation (HOLC) was created. HOLC mortgages had low interest rates and allowed for families to gradually gain equity while paying down their loans (Tough 1951, 326). To assess risk, the HOLC considered the quality and condition of the home as well as the quality of surrounding homes. State government licensing agencies established a "code of ethics" that prohibited real estate agents from selling homes to Black families in White neighborhoods. The HOLC, then, hired real estate agents already beholden to national ethics codes around maintaining racial segregation, to conduct property appraisals. Of course, upon assessing risk, these appraisals took into consideration the racial composition of a given neighborhood. Residential redlining, coined in the 1960s but in existence long before, is a form of mortgage lending discrimination that denies loans to communities or individuals based on race. The term itself references the practice of lending institutions marking largely Black and poor communities in red on maps so as to flag them as undesirable (Mendez et al. 2011, 103). Color-coded maps were created to represent every metropolitan area in the country. Areas perceived as either safe or least risky were colored green and those deemed unsafe or riskier were colored red (Rothstein 2017). A neighborhood was colored red if Black people lived in it, regardless of the socioeconomic standing of the neighborhood. Thus, homeowners living in red neighborhoods were unlikely to be rescued by HOLC and many families in Black communities were forced to foreclose on their homes—creating entire communities where people were forced to abandon their dreams of home ownership. These practices play an essential role in the shaping of neighborhoods' racial composition, development, community health, and wealth attainment (Mendez et al. 2011). Federal and state regulators allowed the banking and insurance industries to deny loans to homeowners in non-White neighborhoods (Rothstein 2019). Banks would not finance the construction of houses or issue mortgages to Black people in search of home ownership. Not only did the Federal Housing Association (FHA), established in the 1930s, and the Veterans Administration (VA) refuse to insure mortgages for Black families wanting to live in White neighborhoods, they refused mortgages to White families in designated

Black areas—thus, maintaining racial housing segregation. The FHA developed and implemented racialized home-appraisal standards and criteria that favored Whites, whereby only all-White neighborhoods rendered the most promising conditions for Whites with respect to acquisition of mortgages, business loans, and other forms of credit that Blacks were barred from (Simms 2019, 56).

During the years following World War II, the FHA and the VA subsidized the development of entire subdivisions to house returning veterans and other working-class residents on a Whites-only basis. To guide the work of real estate agents, the FHA provided them with an underwriting manual of sorts. Real estate agents were instructed that developments could only be built within areas populated by people belonging to "the same racial and social classes"; they were prohibited from constructing developments in proximity to Black neighborhoods out of fear of "infiltration of inharmonious racial" groups. Moreover, the FHA discouraged banks from providing loans to any urban neighborhoods and encouraged home ownership within suburban neighborhoods. The effects of these policies are still seen today. While White working- and middle-class families were able to build wealth through home ownership, Black families were largely excluded from home ownership—relying on renting and less able to build wealth or get out of debt. The long-term effects of this are seen in rates of wealth, educational opportunities, access to home ownership, down payments on homes, and the ability to transform one's assets to future generations (Oliver and Shapiro 2006). Socioeconomic inequity found in lower-income Black communities stems from insufficient access to resources that would otherwise yield upward social mobility; for example, inadequate public-school funding and resources in predominately non-White communities have gone ignored in public policy and further confine these groups to the lower class. Prolonged deprivation of resources in highly concentrated areas of poverty, inevitably yields significant health and wellness issues that affect overall ability and mortality (Massey 2017, 800–1).

By the time the Fair Housing Act of 1968 was passed, banning racial discrimination in the sale or rental of housing, the major residential patterns that we continue to see today were well established (Massey 2015, 571; Rothstein 2019). At the time of its passing, levels of Black residential segregation were extremely high and Black people were considered the most segregated group in the United States (Massey 2015, 571). Also important to note is that the passing of the FHA was an intentional attempt to settle protests in response to Martin Luther King Jr.'s assassination on April 4, 1968. Unfortunately, this was widely ineffective as government enforcement was not held responsible for reinforcing these declarations. Despite these policies having been outlawed, Whites continued to benefit from them. Black families remain largely unable to transform income into wealth in order to provide a cushion for future generations, while White families have had the benefit of decades of wealth accretion.

Real Estate

Throughout the 1950s and beyond, a process known as blockbusting resulted in rapid racial turnover in White neighborhoods. "Blockbusting" is the practice of real estate agents' aggressive, negative solicitation of owned unit listings by emphasizing looming "racial change" in a given area, implying that this change will negatively impact housing values. These real estate agents, or investors, frighten Whites into selling their homes at lower rates and proceed to sell those properties at higher prices to Blacks (Aalbers 2006, 1066). The objective was to scare White homeowners living in borderline Black-White neighborhoods out of their homes once Black families began moving into White neighborhoods. Real estate agents would do this by using phrases like "Negro invasion" in reference to the illusionary collapse of Whites' property values. Other tactics included hiring Black women to push baby carriages through White neighborhoods, paying Black men to drive through White neighborhoods while listening to loud music, and hiring Black men to accompany agents as they knocked on doors asking if homes were for sale. Additionally, speculators would post ads in Black newspapers of homes that were not even for sale to encourage Black people to walk around White areas that had been targeted for blockbusting (Rothstein 2017, 2019; Aalbers 2006).

While benefiting real estate agents, this resulted in massive racial turnover—something commonly referred to as "White flight"—and contributed to the segregation of the Black middle class. Contrary to the message being pushed, property values actually increased when Black families moved into White areas as a direct result of inflated pricing. Eventually, panicked White homeowners would sell their homes at deep discounts. Because most Black families could not qualify for FHA loans, they purchased them by way of installment plans, unable to accrue equity on the homes. Unable to pay the inflated price of homes, Black families were forced to either foreclose or face eviction; a single missed payment could result in eviction. The FHA would, then, use this as proof that property values would decrease if Black families moved in, thus further contributing to predatory and discriminatory lending practices.

Real estate agents attempted to justify barring Black homeowners from White neighborhoods under the guise of preventing declining property values; the few Black families that did enter White neighborhoods often had higher socioeconomic status than their White neighbors. To this end, statistical data counter FHA claims and reveals that integration actually increased property values. This was largely in part to Black families being forced to pay higher prices for their homes. The FHA's discriminatory redlining policies created conditions in which the limited presence of Black families actually prevented the fall of housing values. A 1948 FHA report supports this in finding that "the infiltration of Negro owner-occupants has tended to appreciate property values and neighborhood stability" (cited in Rothstein 2017, 94). Despite this, the FHA continued their race-based housing policies for another decade.

In neighborhoods experiencing integration, property values did eventually decrease. This was not the result of Black home ownership, but rather the result of racist housing policies and the movement of White families out of neighborhoods that had been flagged as "turning." Charging Black people with above-market prices for their homes, then blocking them from FHA loans created situations in which Black families were more likely to default on their loans. Moreover, neighborhoods that had been flagged as having an increasing presence of Black families or areas that bordered Black-White areas were targeted by predatory policies such as blockbusting. As more and more White families fled these neighborhoods and Black families defaulted on their loans, neighborhood conditions decreased as did property values. To further contextualize, between 1999–2004 Black loan applicants in Philadelphia County, Pennsylvania, were nearly two times more likely to be denied a mortgage loan in comparison to their White counterparts (Mendez et al. 2011). Regardless of these realities, fear of deteriorating neighborhoods continues to be at the center of White flight and resistance to integration.

Government-Sanctioned White Violence

Despite the 1948 Supreme Court ruling determining that racially restrictive covenants were not enforceable, homeowner groups insisted that their covenants gave them the right to evict and exclude Black families from White communities. Throughout the 20th century, in White communities across the country, Black families endured vandalism, arson, cross burnings, fire bombings, racial epithets, and more when they moved into White neighborhoods. These acts were often tolerated and promoted by local police, which helped to maintain the systematic segregation of Blacks from Whites across the nation. In some communities, police would stand by as rocks were thrown, crosses were burned, and homes were vandalized, and some police officers would even encourage the mob participants.

State-sanctioned violence was one way in which the government maintained and perpetuated racial-residential segregation. The failure of police officers to protect the Black families whom they are charged to protect, coupled with their encouragement of mob violence toward Black people, is just another way in which the government sanctioned the segregation of Black families from White families. Here, too, we acknowledge the ways in which the systems of law enforcement and housing intersect to the detriment of Black families.

Policing and Neighborhood Segregation

We cannot understand the policing of Black communities in contemporary urban (and suburban) spaces without, first, recognizing the ways in which Black people have *always* been surveilled and controlled by law enforcement. The police have historically participated in enforcing discriminatory laws—treating White citizens as those who need protection and Black citizens as those unworthy of civil liberties and equal treatment. Despite the dismantling of Jim Crow segregation, de facto segregation persists and perpetuates a punitive relationship between non-White communities and the police (Bass 2001). The monitoring and policing of Black people is nothing new in America, the supposed land of the free. Informal slave patrols were created to monitor, terrorize, and control the movement of slaves, newly freed as well as free Black people (Reichel 1999; Williams and Murphy 1990). Jim Crow segregation, the creation of public housing, and urban ghettos is yet another deliberate effort by the federal government to control and surveil the lives of Black people. Since the first African slave ships arrived in America, Black people have been controlled and surveilled in public spaces. Of course, the Black community is not the only group to have experienced high levels of state-sanctioned surveillance or violence. However, no other racial group has experienced the sustained, high levels of neighborhood segregation that Black people have (Massey and Denton 1993).

As Black migration from the South to the North during the Great Migration surged, so did the regulation of Black people in public space. As race riots broke out in response to the growing Black population (Massey and Denton 1993), federal policy was developed to encourage White flight to the suburbs and restrict Black presence in White spaces as a means of remedying the presumed issues (Rothstein 2019). While White residents certainly participated in maintaining segregation between races, law enforcement upheld and implemented formal and informal social control on many levels—playing a significant role in residential segregation in northern cities (Sugrue 1996).

Once the "War on Drugs" began in the 1970s, Black urban ghettos had become a permanent fixture of American life—largely the result of discriminatory race-based federal policy, but also reinforced by White residents and local police forces. The policies implemented during the Nixon administration, in association with the War on Drugs, gave rise to discriminatory laws and policing—all aimed at creating race-based public policy that directly targeted the Black community. The drug war, too, gave rise to the increased militarization of policing, which we see more commonly now (Chambliss 1994). Additional violations of civil liberties upheld by federal policy include racial profiling, "Terry stops," and stop and frisk—all highly racialized policies that provide officers discretion in targeting and profiling Black people. Terry stops (referring to the landmark Terry v. Ohio case of 1968) are another way of discouraging integration and keeping Black people out of White spaces by stopping and questioning Black people found in largely White spaces. These stops are not limited to poor, Black people coming from urban ghettos, but more frequently target middle- and high-income Black people who live and work in White spaces (Capers 2009). In fact, most Terry stops involved individuals who were neither carrying contraband nor engaged in criminal activity. In 2006 alone, nine out of ten stop-and-frisk encounters in the state of New York resulted in no summons being served because individuals were not engaged in any unlawful activities. Policies such as these not only contribute to the overpolicing of Black people in urban environments, but they uphold and perpetuate the segregation of public and private space as well.

The 1980s gave rise to what is commonly referred to as "broken-windows policing." This practice is based on the premise that low-level quality-of-life environmental factors such as graffiti, potholes, litter, panhandling, and broken windows are signs of neighborhood disorganization. This is presumed to be a signal for criminals that little informal social control is present, as well as a cue for police that the re-engagement of community is necessary (Kelling and Wilson 1982). This led officers to "crack down" on low-level offenses under the assumption that it would decrease higher-level infractions to come; this type of policing was later referred to as "zero-tolerance policing." This gave rise to Black people being stopped and frisked more often for doing nothing at all.

Born out of a history of racial discrimination, the drug war, stop and frisk, racial profiling, Terry stops, and zero-tolerance policing are all forms of federal policy that uphold White supremacy and race-based neighborhood segregation. The role of police in maintaining and perpetuating residential segregation is evident, as is the extent to which Black people are overpoliced in neighborhoods (Fagan, West, and Hollan 2003). The summative consequence of punitive policing in segregated, urban environments is that these policies permit the disproportionate policing of Black people in all spaces—in their homes, in their cars, on the streets, in shopping centers, in schools, and any other space where it has been socially sanctioned that "Black people do not belong."

CHAPTER 4

Contemporary Racial-Residential Segregation

> If you're calling for an end to unrest, but not calling out police brutality, not calling for health care as a human right, not calling for an end to housing discrimination, all you're asking for is the continuation of quiet oppression.
>
> —Alexandria Ocasio-Cortez

The bulk of scholarship and literary work related to racial inequality within the United States often lends itself to more recognizable issues, such as income inequality and policy matters including affirmative action. However, a trend has emerged over the last forty years or so in which scholars have turned their attention to residential segregation as a critical, contributing factor to Black-White inequality plaguing American society (Charles 2003; Emerson, Yancey, and Chai 2001; Massey and Denton 1993). In American metropolitan areas, segregation amplifies and exacerbates social and economic problems, leaving African Americans not only economically disadvantaged but also often concentrated in and restricted to poor neighborhoods with limited access to economic opportunities such as homeownership, social mobility, higher-paying jobs, and quality schools otherwise abundant in wealthier areas (Massey and Denton 1993; Wilkes and Iceland 2004). Racial-residential segregation creates a ripple effect, multiplying socioeconomic barriers that shape the very lives of African Americans.

While there has been a steady decrease in racial-residential segregation (Fischer 2003; Glaeser and Vigdor 2001, 2012), Black-White segregation remains persistently high in most American metropolises (Charles 2003; Emerson, Yancey, and Chai 2001; Iceland and Wilkes 2006; Massey and Denton 1993; Sui and Wu 2006). Explanations for persisting high levels of racial segregation vary. Some social scientists argue that socioeconomic differences among groups is responsible for residential segregation, while others point to persisting prejudice and discrimination by individuals and institutions within housing and lending markets (e.g., Charles 2003; Iceland and Wilkes 2006). Scholars have also argued that the neighborhood preferences of individuals and families play a critical role in enforcing and maintaining segregation (Bobo and Zubrinksy 1996; Krysan and Bader 2007; Semyonov et al. 2007). While scholars debate the exact mechanisms responsible for generating and sustaining segregation, there is little doubt that racial segregation harms Black people across socioeconomic classes. Ongoing dialogue and debate surrounding White advantages in the housing market highlight the importance of race, class, and residential preferences.

Data highlight discrepancies in individual residential preferences as they concern racial-neighborhood composition. Previous studies indicate that Blacks prefer to live in integrated neighborhoods, while Whites prefer to live in predominantly White neighborhoods (e.g., Farley et al. 1978; Zubrinsky and Bobo 1996). Considering Whites wield more privilege and power in the housing market at all levels, it is of no surprise that White preference reflects what we see across the nation—Whites living in predominately White neighborhoods. A culmination of distinctive Black and White preferences, racism and discrimination, housing and lending discrimination (Massey and Denton 1993; Yinger 1995), and Black fear of White neighborhoods due to hostility (Bobo and Zubrinksy 1996; Krysan 2002b; Krysan and Bader 2007; Semyonov, Glickman, and Krysan 2007) all create additional barriers to integration.

Social scientists continue to debate whether race exercises an independent effect on residential preferences, or whether there are other nonracial factors responsible for shaping residential preferences. Scholars focused on residential preferences as a determining factor assert that residential segregation is not only a result of economic differentials and discrimination, but that it is also the result of preferences for different types of neighborhood composition. One confounding factor of residential preferences is that Whites may prefer White neighborhoods because they associate them with better housing stock, better services (such as schools), and fewer social problems, rather than a preference for living among Whites per se. The converse may be true in terms of White avoidance of Black or Hispanic *neighborhoods* as opposed to Blacks or Hispanics *as people*. Some scholars contend that part of the reason Whites prefer neighborhoods with fewer Blacks may not be antipathy toward Black neighbors simply because they are Black, but rather because they may associate Black neighborhoods with poorer housing stock, poorer services, and more social problems (Ellen 2000; Emerson, Yancey, and Chai 2001; Harris 2001). To this end, Whites may avoid neighborhoods with many non-Whites because of the link between neighborhood-racial composition and neighborhood conditions and social problems; this, with the added problem of racialized stigmas, reinforce such ideals (Ellen 2000).

The growing interest in racial-residential segregation as a contributing factor in racial inequality was brought forth by the publications of Massey and Denton's *American Apartheid* (1993) and William Julius Wilson's *The Truly Disadvantaged* (1987). Massey, Denton, Wilson, and many other scholars highlight the many consequences of segregation and isolation especially for African Americans. The general consensus is that residential segregation serves as a barrier for Black people by isolating them from well-paying jobs, quality schools, low-crime environments, and access to crucial social networks (Brooks-Gunn et al. 1993; Massey 1990; Massey and Denton 1993, Rosenbaum 1995; Rosenbaum, Reynolds, and Deluca 2002; Wagmiller 2007). Moreover, studies on racial-residential segregation elevate our understanding of "ghetto poverty" (Jargowsky 1994, 1996; Massey 1990; Massey and Denton 1993; Wilson 1987). While many scholars have added to our fundamental understanding of this issue, Massey and Denton (1993) argue that sociologists have failed to thoroughly consider racial-residential segregation as a leading factor in the construction of the "Black ghetto," particularly as it concerns the intentional practices of individuals, institutions, and private sectors aimed at maintaining racial segregation.

Explaining Segregation

Three general explanations for the persistent segregation of American neighborhoods are identified by scholars of segregation as the spatial-assimilation model, the place-stratification model, and individual residential preferences. Each of these models serve to contribute to and further overall discussions and understanding of racial segregation. Beginning with spatial assimilation, we discuss the nuances of each model and its contributions.

SPATIAL ASSIMILATION

The spatial-assimilation model is premised on the idea that as racial and ethnic groups increase their socioeconomic status, they move away from the central city and into the suburbs (e.g., Alba et al. 1999; Alba and Logan 1991; Emerson et al. 2001; Iceland and Wilkes 2006). This theoretical position presupposes that individuals are inclined to leave ethnic neighborhoods in search of residential areas of greater socioeconomic status. Simply put, this model argues that segregation is the result of economic differentials between Blacks and Whites and segregation persists because people live where they can afford to live (Farley et al. 1997). The viability of this model has been called into question as numerous studies have found that high-income Blacks are as equally segregated from high-income Whites as low-income Blacks are from low-income Whites (e.g., Adelman 2004, 2005; Denton and Massey 1988; South and Crowder 1997). South and Crowder (1997), too, recognize that while greater income increases a person's chances of moving to the suburbs, they also point out that socioeconomic status does not explain relocation and settlement into the suburbs. Researchers maintain that there are several other factors worthy of consideration with respect to Black, Brown, and immigrant groups' residential patterns, particularly as they pertain to Blacks and other people of color. African Americans have historically had a difficult time moving into suburban areas (Alba et al. 1999; Alba and Nee 2003), a pattern that continues for low- to moderate- income Blacks. Massey and Mullan (1984) examined differences among Hispanic and Black assimilation into the suburbs, and Blacks were much less able to translate income or status into relocation to White, suburban neighborhoods than Hispanics were (see also Alba and Logan 1999). Even though middle-class Blacks in the United States have more favorable residential outcomes than poor Blacks, and often live in the suburbs, they continue to live in poorer neighborhoods than most Whites (Adelman 2004; Pattillo-McCoy 1999; Pattillo 2005, 2007). On average, Blacks and Whites have different levels of assets and wealth across class statuses based on income (Oliver and Shapiro 1995); Blacks remain limited in their ability to attain housing in middle-class suburban areas, even when they can afford it. Socioeconomic status aside, Blacks are less likely to relocate to White, suburban neighborhoods (South and Crowder 1997).

The spatial assimilation perspective fails to adequately account for race because it overlooks the very fact that racial segregation is present and persistent among middle-class and affluent Blacks (Adelman 2004; Denton and Massey 1988; Krysan 2002a). This perspective remains contested because, even with existing economic differences between Blacks and Whites, economic differences alone cannot exhaustively explain racial-residential segregation. It is important to consider the role of institutional and individual discrimination and racism (Adelman 2005; Farley et al. 1997).

PLACE STRATIFICATION

The place-stratification model was developed to recognize the role of prejudice and discrimination within banking, lending, and the real estate market. This model closely examines the role of individual and institutional forces in maintaining segregation (e.g., Charles 2003; Iceland and Wilkes 2006). Scholars drawing on the place-stratification model emphasize the role of racism and discrimination in racial-residential segregation and stress that, regardless of socioeconomic status, race remains an ever-present factor, particularly for African Americans (Krysan 2002a; Massey and Denton 1993; South and Crowder 1997). Opportunities for better housing outside urban ghettos play a key role in the spatial-assimilation process. It is necessary to acknowledge that Whites have not been discriminated against by housing and lending practices in the same ways that Blacks have been systematically disadvantaged. Institutional factors leading to segregation and limited mobility for Blacks include discrimination in the real estate and lending industries (Charles 2003; Massey and Denton 1993).

Yinger (1995) found that, when all other factors, such as income and credit history were equal, Blacks were treated kindly by real estate agents on their first visit but were less likely to be encouraged for a return visit and were given less information about available homes (Ondrich et al. 2000; Ondrich et al. 2003; Turner 1992). Yinger also acknowledged discrimination in the lending market in finding that, again, when all factors apart from race were equal, Blacks were more likely to be turned down for loans in comparison to Whites. This calls attention to institutionalized practices that maintain and perpetuate segregation by steering Whites and Blacks in different directions. Although recent studies suggest that institutional discrimination has declined to some extent, we find that racially discriminatory practices persist both overtly and covertly and continue to render very real consequences at the expense of Black people (Glaeser and Vigdor 2001, 2012).

INDIVIDUAL HOUSING PREFERENCES

Individual preferences related to the racial composition of one's neighborhood may be identified as fitting within the place-stratification model—considering discrimination at the individual level and the ways in which individual choices about neighborhoods maintain segregation. However, this notion is contested under the premise that it is a third, separate, explanation for segregation and stands alone as a distinct theoretical position. The residential-preferences model is based on the notion that residential segregation is the result of not only economic differentials and discrimination but also preferences for different types of neighborhoods with varying racial compositions. Even in the absence of housing discrimination, such preferences may work to maintain segregation (Fossett 2006).

Adelman (2005) finds that while White people often endorse the principle of living among Blacks, their behaviors did not reflect such attitudes. A major issue within the residential-preferences debate revolves around White Americans' avoidance of racially mixed neighborhoods because they do not want to live with non-Whites, and whether nonracial factors motivate such choices. In search of more clarity, researchers seek to examine whether race has an independent effect on residential preferences beyond factors often stereotypically associated with Black neighborhoods, such as social problems, poverty, and poor housing. Several researchers conclude that it does, in fact, yield an independent effect (e.g., Charles 2000; Emerson et al. 2001; Massey and Denton 1993; Meyerhoffer 2016; Zubrinsky and Bobo 1996), while other scholars (e.g., Clark 1986; Harris 2001) argue that once the factors associated with race are controlled, race does not have an independent effect on whether people live in certain areas.

Those who argue that race is independent of neighborhood conditions do so on the premise that preferences are rooted in White racism and Black fear of White hostility (Bobo and Zubrinksy 1996; Charles 2003). As such, preferences reflect some level of racial discrimination on behalf of White residents and are one way in which racial-residential segregation remains. Krysan (2002a) argues that White avoidance of Black neighborhoods has racist underpinnings that override perceptions of job opportunities and quality of education. Preference patterns rooted in racial hostility further enable racial division through social interaction and social institutions, and, at least partly, reflect racially charged attitudes regarding residential decisions.

Scholars have also made the argument that it is not necessarily Black neighbors that Whites take issue with; rather, it is the effect of having a large population of Black neighbors concentrated within the same area (see Ellen 2000; and Harris 2001). Quillian (1995) acknowledges the importance of the size of a subordinate group relative to the dominant group, arguing that an increase in anti-Black prejudice is contingent upon an increase in Black population size. Dixon (2006) echoes that the issue is not the presence of *any* racial minority group, but that Whites react more negatively to the presence of large groups of Black neighbors in particular; that while living near Hispanics or Asians reduces White prejudice, living near large groups of Blacks actually heightens White prejudice. Lieberson (1980) also recognizes the importance of group size in observing that the ability of Blacks to move out of poor neighborhoods and into ones of greater socioeconomic status decreases in areas consisting of relatively large Black populations. Furthermore, the size of the Black population in a given area serves as a barrier to mobility into the suburbs because of the perceived threat to Whites and, thus, increases discrimination (South and Deane 1993). In a later study, Quillian and Pager (2001) point out that even after controlling for measures related to neighborhood characteristics, such as crime rates, the percentage of young Black men in a given neighborhood is strongly associated with perceptions of crime. To be clear, Whites are more likely to leave a neighborhood experiencing an increase in non-White residents and are especially likely to leave if there are multiple non-White racial groups (Crowder 2000). Krysan (1998, 2002a), as well as others (e.g., Adelman 2005; Emerson et al. 2001; Massey and Denton 1993), argue that while race is not the only factor driving residential preferences, it continues to play a significant role in the residential decision-making process. Krysan (1998, 2002a) addresses the relevancy of class by demonstrating that Whites perceived economically prosperous areas that were predominantly Black as less desirable than equally, or even less, prosperous White neighborhoods; this further cements the reality that race plays a leading role.

To control for proxy variables, several scholars (Farley et al. 1978; Krysan 1998 and 2002a; Meyerhoffer 2015, 2016; Meyerhoffer and Kenty-Drane 2018) have employed hypothetical neighborhood "show cards" that represent neighborhoods of various racial compositions. Respondents are instructed to select the hypothetical neighborhood show card they would most prefer to reside in out of a stack of show cards. These studies reveal that Whites' overall preference is for predominantly White neighborhoods. Harris (2001) makes the case that it is not only Whites who are averse to Black neighborhoods, but Blacks, too, share this aversion. Harris finds that both Whites and Blacks prefer White neighborhoods because predominantly Black neighborhoods are, generally, associated with high crime rates, poverty, poor education systems, and other perceived social problems (2001; Ellen 2000). Overall, scholars have found that Blacks prefer relatively high levels of out-group contact with Whites in their neighborhoods, while Whites prefer predominantly White neighborhoods (e.g., Bobo and Zubrinsky 1996; Charles 2003; Farley et al. 1978; Krysan et al. 2009; Zubrinsky and Bobo 1996). Whites' preference to live in predominately White neighborhoods remains a dominant factor in shaping racial-residential segregation. Individual social location and racial biases toward other races influence the home search process (Meyerhoffer 2015). Moreover, Whites with greater income focus more on the preservation of property values and neighborhood safety; this is suggestive of the notion that Whites, whether consciously or subconsciously, presume that non-White neighbors threaten the preservation of these entities regardless of whether such is the case. Several perspectives have sought to explain the aforesaid White aversion to non-White neighborhoods, especially predominantly Black neighborhoods—these include the pure-race and racial-proxy perspectives, on the one hand, and race-associated and racial-stereotyping perspectives, on the other.

PURE-RACE AND RACIAL-PROXY PERSPECTIVES

Some scholars are of the position that racial composition is the single-most driving factor of neighborhood preferences, regardless of the socioeconomic conditions or levels of social problems in a given neighborhood. From this perspective, scholars stress that Whites prefer White neighborhoods and are averse to Black neighborhoods because of race per se (Charles 2000; Emerson et al. 2001; Krysan and Bader 2007; Krysan et. al. 2009; Lewis et. al. 2011; Zubrinsky and Bobo 1996).

In contrast, other scholars insist that preferences are not based on race per se, but rather that race simply serves as a proxy variable for the socioeconomic status and social organization of a neighborhood (Ellen 2000; Harris 2001). To this extent, it is argued that one reason Whites prefer neighborhoods with few Blacks may not be due to an aversion toward Black neighbors because they are Black, but rather because they likely associate Black neighborhoods with poorer housing stock, poorer services, and prevalent social problems (Farley et al. 1994; Timberlake 2000). Along this same vein, through the race-based neighborhood stereotyping perspective, Ellen (2000) argues that negative perceptions toward predominately Black neighborhoods are not reflective of Black people as individuals, but, rather, they are linked to negative stereotypes people have of Black neighborhoods.

RACE-ASSOCIATED AND RACIAL STEREOTYPING PERSPECTIVES

Both the race-associated and racial stereotyping perspectives speak to the difficulty scholars have with separating race from class and racial stereotypes. This proves particularly true with respect to the race-associated perspective (Krysan 1998 and 2002a). The race-associated perspective underscores a failure to discern between perceptions of Blacks as people, the actual conditions of Black neighborhoods, and perceptions of Black neighborhoods (Krysan 2002a, but see also Bobo and Zubrinsky 1996; Charles 2000). Farley et al. (1994) speak to this in their finding that anti-Black stereotypes are strongly associated with White avoidance of Black neighborhoods, regardless of the actual condition of the neighborhoods (see also Quillian and Pager 2001). Other studies attribute racial stereotypes of Black neighborhoods as being strong predictors of White residential preferences (Bobo and Zubrinsky 1996; Charles 2000; Emerson, et al. 2001; and Timberlake 2000), again, regardless of the actual conditions of those neighborhoods (Quillian and Pager 2001).

Race, too, yields positive and negative stereotyping related to quality-of-life conditions in neighborhoods (Quillian and Pager 2001), perhaps even subconsciously in the minds of residents evaluating White and non-White residential areas. To this end, it is possible that people's perceptions of proxy factors, such as school quality and crime, are colored by respective perceptions of race. Furthermore, it is possible that their attitudes toward racial and ethnic groups reflect the associations they make between race and presumed residential social problems, as well as socioeconomic status.

It is necessary to acknowledge that explanations for residential segregation are not mutually exclusive. An increase in income generally leads to greater residential opportunities (Alba et al. 1999; Alba and Logan 1991). However, non-White racial groups, particularly Black people, experience greater challenges when moving into the suburbs regardless of socioeconomic status (Iceland and Wilkes 2006). In fact, poor White people are more likely to live in higher-income neighborhoods in comparison to middle- and higher- income Black people. These perspectives are further complicated by the role of residential preferences in which socioeconomic status, racial composition, and discrimination are significant factors (Farley et al. 1997). That is, while socioeconomic status serves as one determining factor in residential location, Blacks often live in predominantly Black neighborhoods, regardless of class, for reasons related to both persisting discriminatory practices and Black fear of White hostility (Bobo and Zubrinksy 1996; Krysan 2002b; Semyonov et al. 2007; Krysan and Bader 2007).

SOCIAL-STRUCTURAL SORTING

Finally, despite decreasing overt discrimination, housing segregation persists. As Maria Krysan and Kyle Crowder argue, in *Cycle of Segregation: Social Processes and Residential Stratification* (2017), housing segregation is so entrenched in American life that individual perceptions of neighborhoods have been fundamentally altered. They make this argument by analyzing the search for housing itself and the many steps along the way, often littered with confusion, inaccurate information, and heuristics that cloud the judgments of those in search of housing. Krysan and Crowder push back against notions that economic differentials are what segregate America, arguing that perceptions of affordability are colored through an already-racialized lens—thus, a person of color perceiving a White neighborhood as out of one's price range without actual knowledge of housing costs in that area impacts the likelihood that they will even look at a home in that neighborhood. Moreover, building off the work of previous scholars who argue that White people prefer racially homogenous neighborhoods and will remove neighborhoods with sizable minority population from their list of options, they find that White people do not consider these neighborhoods in the first place and that cognitive shortcuts about minority neighborhoods color their perceptions long before the home ownership process even starts. This book's theoretical argument is essential to understanding how racial-residential segregation functions like most systems in America, as they posit; discrimination in the housing market, they suggest, is embedded in the very fabric of the United states and the circuitry of how people search for homes.

Segregation, Government Policy, and the Role of Policing

This chapter covers several theoretical frameworks through which racial-residential segregation is examined. While contemporary residential segregation is due to a number of individual-level and government-level policies, it is important to remember that when scholars talk about residential segregation, they often refer to it as de facto segregation. De facto segregation is not created nor upheld by government policy; rather, it "just happens." De jure segregation is the result of policies and practices that are legally recognized and enforced; an example of such being Jim Crow segregation. Rothstein (2019) asserts that the very notion of de facto neighborhood segregation perpetuates neighborhood segregation because if segregation is, in fact, de facto, it would be unconstitutional to take explicit steps to reduce it. However, segregation is not, and never has been, de facto. In fact, our federal, state, and local governments have a long history of establishing explicitly racialized policies that generate the very segregation we continue to see in our neighborhoods and school systems to date. Moreover, neighborhood segregation is the result of not only federal government policy and discrimination in the housing market but the institution of law enforcement as well. For example, Black families attempting to move into White neighborhoods were subject to bombings and violence at the hands of White mobs during the earlier stages of residential integration. In response, police were encouraged not to intervene nor protect Black families despite such grotesque displays of White violence (Massey 2015). Moreover, police enforcement prioritized the maintenance and preservation of White racial homogeneity within neighborhoods as their utmost responsibility—and in doing so, chose not to protect fellow Americans they swore to protect. To this end, Rothstein (2019) argues that because the police were paid by the government to do so, violence induced by these White mobs cannot be considered de facto segregation by definition. To be clear, racial-residential segregation is the product of racially explicit policies that were legally sanctioned at federal, state, and local levels—policies so powerful that they continue to uphold and perpetuate contemporary neighborhood segregation. As we see in the next chapter, this affects not only how people access housing but also the quality of education they receive.

CHAPTER 5

Whitewashed, Segregated Education

When young people are in crisis, that's the moment we bring them in closer, not the moment we try to push them away.

—Monique Morris

The *Brown v. Board of Education* decision of 1954 determined that racial segregation in public schools is unconstitutional. Despite this, public schools remain more segregated by race today than at any point in roughly the last forty years (Rothstein 2019). Public education in the United States perpetually disadvantages children of color in several ways. Public-school educators are primarily White women (Sleeter and McLaren 1995); they not only lack adequate preparation for teaching students of color (Cross 2003) but also fail to include curricula and pedagogy that veers away from White and European content and style (Gay 1995; Boyer and Baptiste 1996). This creates an environment in which White students continue to have an advantage in American public schools, while students of color are neglected. Swartz (1992) argues that mainstream pedagogical practices in American public schools are inappropriate for students of color and purposefully uphold and perpetuate White supremacy. Critical race theorists refer to traditional school curricula as "master scripting"—this phrase refers to dominant culture controlling the content and delivery of curricula. Master scripting serves to silence the voices and experiences of African Americans and is employed at both the institutional and individual level (Blanchett 2006). This produces racist trends that can be found throughout many public schools. For example, African American history is commonly taught as an elective, Black historical figures are intentionally excluded from most disciplines, and Black students are not able to "see themselves" in their education.

Whitewashed curricula are taught to students of color predominantly by White women who often maintain deficit views of children of color—due, in part, to housing segregation. This fosters hostile environments for Black children in which microaggressions remain unchecked. Black students are, consequently, less likely to be mentored and supported by their teachers. Cross (2003) found that neither the race of the teacher, nor the racial composition of the school, nor the teacher's ability to teach in multiracial spaces is considered in determining teacher quality. This is increasingly concerning as America's teaching workforce becomes increasingly White. Using National Center for Education Statistics data, in 2003 Cross determined that 86.6 percent of the teaching faculty were White and that this rate is projected to increase annually. Not surprisingly, those responsible for preparing teachers for work—teacher educators—are disproportionately White. Teacher educators are, therefore, unable to effectively prepare prospective teachers for entering non-White school systems and perpetuate a divide between staff and the student body. Despite calls for inclusion, culturally responsive curricula, and diversity standards, teacher preparation programs continue to graduate educators that are ill-prepared to effectively teach Black and other students of color (Blanchett 2006). Providing culturally responsive curricula is vital and will likely improve student learning across racial divides (Darling-Hammond 2004). Negative perceptions of Black students, as well as other students of color, play out in the learning environment and pose a threat to the very lives of Black students. These destructive perceptions include a number of factors: perceived levels of "deviance" exhibited by a student, the violence these students are subjected to, their capacity for success, and their placement into special education programs (Sleeter 1993).

Neighborhood Segregation = Segregated Public Schools

Segregation in American public schools is a natural consequence of neighborhood racial segregation. Public schools are often funded by property taxes, which results in fewer resources in poor schools in the form of guidance counselors, social workers, and nurses. Over the last thirty years, urban public schools have become overwhelmingly populated by students of color (Piana 2000, in Cross 2003)—a trend that was projected to reach 48 percent by 2020 (Pallas, Natriello, and McDill 1989, in Cross 2003), and now, in 2022 has reached approximately 55% ("Fatal Force" 2022). The term "urban school" carries with it a host of stereotypes that suggest they are in poor condition, underfunded, produce underperforming students, and are composed of a predominately non-White student body. Inadequate staffing, insufficient resources, poor infrastructure, overcrowding, dilapidated facilities, lack of academic rigor, and outdated curricula are all commonly associated with urban schooling (Wright and Alenuma 2007). In addition to schools with large Black and Brown populations being underfunded (Blanchett 2006), urban schools also disproportionately employ uncredentialled or underprepared teachers that implement less rigorous curricula in schools that tend to have physical structures in need of significant repair (Darling-Hammond 2004; National Research Council 2002). Alternatively, White students are exposed to more rigorous curricula (Brantlinger 2003), have highly educated and credentialed teachers, attend schools that are predominantly White, and are less likely to be placed in special education programs (Blanchett et al. 2005, Robinson and Grant-Thomas 2004). Students attending schools in high-poverty areas experience higher rates of turnover in staffing, have limited access to technology, are afforded few foreign-language programs, receive little to no education specialists, and are offered fewer advanced classes (Kozol 2004, Orfield and Lee 2004). A growing shortage of teachers in the United States, too, poses a particular threat in communities deemed most unstable due to its impact on teaching quality (Zhang and Zeller 2016). In 2012, researchers Ingersoll, Merrill, and May cited that between 40 percent to 50 percent of teachers will leave their place of work within the first five years and 9.5 percent will leave before the end of their first year. Ingersoll (2004) employs the term "the revolving-door effect" to describe the rampant cycle of teacher turnover rates in schools considered "at-risk," in which these schools are in near-constant search of new hires to replace those that quit. This trend—of revolving novice teachers—incites a stream of inexperienced educators that are ill-equipped to effectively instruct, which proves to be particularly rampant in predominately Black communities. New teachers entering the field are more likely to be placed in districts considered most needy and provided fewer resources (Zhang and Zeller 2016). Consequently, the student-teacher relationship is often strained as students become increasingly jaded by the cyclical turnover and discouraged from forming personal connections. This also impacts students' ability to network, which can be critical when it comes to the recommendation and advisement portion of the college-application process. A widely known band-aid for the national-teacher shortage is Teach for America (TFA)—a nonprofit organization that funnels new teachers to predominately urban and rural school districts for two-year stints. While having received praise for its work, TFA has also received significant criticism for its educational approach in urban and rural-school districts and overall program efficacy. The two-year term that TFA enforces only further contributes to the issue of teacher turnover and residual effects in already vulnerable communities.

Finally, placement of African American students in general education and special education programs results in what some refer to as second-generation segregation. According to a 2002 study, African American students only make up 14.8 percent of the general student population yet account for 20 percent of the special education population (Losen and Orfield 2002) creating a disproportionate number of Black students in special education programs. Once this disproportionate number of Black students are placed in special education categories, they are less likely to exit special education programs and make achievement gains in comparison to White students in special education programs (U.S. Department of Education 2004). The purpose of special education programs is to provide much-needed educational support for differently abled students with the intent to gradually transition them out of the program and into the general education setting (Blanchett and Shealey 2005). However, rather than provide these supports and prepare students for general education, special education programs have become a form of segregation for poor students and students of color (Civil Rights Project 2001) that serves as a mechanism through which they do not receive equitable education (Losen and Orfield 2002). Burris and Welner (2005) find that when African American students identified as having disabilities are not placed in tracked classes, but are, instead, exposed to rigorous curricula and high expectations, the achievement gap between Black and White students is significantly reduced. Moreover, Harry and Klinger (2006) argue that the higher quality of education that African American students receive in the general education program may decrease the likelihood that they will be placed in a special education program.

Magnet Schools

Alternative schools have a long history in the United States, typically aiming to achieve reform efforts rooted in particular social, political, or religious goals. Magnet schools were birthed out of the 1954 *Brown vs. Board of Education* Supreme Court case whereby districts were mandated to desegregate school systems throughout America. Replacing the term "alternative," with the phrase "magnet schooling" gained popularity in the 1970s when policy-makers were developing plans for desegregation and it was chosen to seem more appealing to students and families (Smrekar 2009; Wright and Alenuma 2007). Magnet schools are public schools that incentivize parents through specialized programs, curricular themes, and instructional methods in the promotion of greater school choice (Archbald 2004; Smrekar 2009). They aim to achieve the following two goals: (1), enhance students' academic performance through distinctive curricula and, (2), enhance the schools' racial and social diversity (West 1994; Wright and Alenuma 2007). Magnet schools experienced significant growth in the 1980s as an alternative for low-income students in the promotion of the school-choice movement, resulting in over half of all magnet schools being situated in low socioeconomic districts (Archbald 2004; Goldring and Smrekar 2002). Magnet schools are funded through state-segregation funds and the Magnet Schools Assistance Program (MSAP). MSAP is a federally funded program that offers three-year grants to qualifying magnet schools and has played a critical role in expansion efforts throughout the United States, providing roughly $100 million to magnet school programs annually. The U.S. Department of Education reports that 53 percent of all large urban districts include magnet school programs as part of their desegregation plans, whereas only 10 percent of suburban districts include such programs (Goldring and Smrekar 2002). Magnet schools tend to market themselves as for the "gifted" in an effort to appeal more to parents and accomplish this through specialized programming and curricula (West 1994). Specialized programs focused on particular subjects, such as technology or STEM, offered at these magnet schools aim to entice White families to enroll their children in urban schools, while drawing non-White families on the premise of integration (Minow 2011). While the efficacy of magnet schools remains contested and studies have shown inconsistent results, they remain highly sought after by families as over 75 percent of all districts offering magnet schools are unable to meet the high demand, resulting in lengthy waitlists (Goldring and Smrekar 2002).

The school-choice movement within the United States is marked as a major development over the past two decades and has received both praise and criticism. Supporters of school choice contend that it "liberates" low-income students from their respective schools, while critics counterargue that it deepens the socioeconomic divide across income stratifications (Archbald 2004, 283). Supporters of school choice are of the view that its framework invokes market-like competition among schools and inadvertently pushes them to improve in their effort to maintain enrollment and retain students (Goldring and Smrekar 2002). Opponents contend that a market-like model further depletes already vulnerable public schools, particularly in marginalized communities. While magnet schools are generally revered as one of the more effective tools for desegregation within school systems, classrooms within these magnet schools remain racially segregated. Contributing factors of continued classroom segregation are identified as the methods employed in assigning students to academic programs—including tracking and grouping students according to ability—and the disciplinary practices that discriminate against non-White students. Black students are disproportionately more likely to be suspended or expelled by school authorities as compared with their White peers, which is in line with the racial biases we see play out in other institutions. Magnet schools stand by this practice by hiding behind the rhetoric of holding high disciplinary standards, serving to compel White families to send their children into urban magnet school districts (West 1994). These sorts of institutionalized practices can be found in contemporary policing and the implicit racial biases of the general public in which Black students and Black neighborhoods are presumedly dangerous solely because they are not White; herein, indirectly implying that White is the standard for safety and academic success. Carla Shedd (2015), in her book *Unequal City: Race, Schools, and Perceptions of Injustice*, documents the real and symbolic harm done to high-school students in school, as they travel to school, and in their communities. Shedd (2015) pushes readers to view schools not only as institutions of education but also engines of social inequality and stratification through the criminalization of children, punitive education, and policies such as "school choice" that only serve to benefit White children at the expense of children of color. Critics, therefore, mock magnet schools as a tool for racial desegregation given the sheer irony of their racially segregated classroom structures and disciplinary practices. The magnet school model perpetuates the narrative of White superiority and, by default, non-White inferiority (West 1994).

Charter Schools

The "Black-White achievement gap" is a term used to describe the learning disparity found when measuring academic achievement among Black students in comparison to their White peers. Herein, Black students generally perform more poorly than White students due to a culmination of several factors. Scholars have identified several such causal factors responsible for this gap, including a lack of curricular rigor, inadequate teacher training programs, inexperienced educators, insufficient school resources, poor health care, and lack of affordable housing. Another causal factor has been identified as a more recent phenomenon—the public charter-school movement (Almond 2012). Charter schools are central to public education reform efforts within the United States and disproportionately impact Black students and families.

Charter schools are publicly funded, K-12 nonsectarian schools that operate under the supervision of local education agencies and are free from many public-school regulations (Almond 2012; Clark et al. 2015). These schools are established on the basis of a contract that a private board holds with a charter authorizer, granting release from any state or district regulation (Clark et al. 2015). Charter schools characteristically differ from traditional public schools in five ways. They have (1) a defined mission statement with a focus on academic performance, (2) a culture of high expectations, (3) a college-forward environment, (4) a focus on standardized tests, and (5) longer school days and extended academic years (Almond 2012). Between 1992 and 1997, roughly five hundred public charter schools were created and have since experienced double-digit growth annually (Almond 2012). These schools are typically located in urban areas and target underachieving students, and serve low-income families that are looking to opt out of a traditional schooling model, resulting in nearly 64 percent of all charter schools being composed of non-White students (Almond 2012). In 2010–2011, Monica Almond found that Black families were seeking public charter schools at an unprecedented rate, nearly double the rate of traditional schooling. This is, perhaps, due in part to racial-residential segregation whereby Whites have significantly greater access to quality school systems and educational resources within their local districts resulting from the access Whiteness affords a predominately White neighborhood composition. In a nationwide study involving 95.4 percent of the U.S. charter-school population, Frankenburg and Lee (2003) found that most charter schools enroll disproportionately high rates of minoritized students, of which Black students comprise the largest subset population. May (2006) found that this trend is connected to parents' perception that charter schools offer enhanced educational experiences and yield greater academic gains than their respective public schools, though data do not indicate this is the case. In fact, research addressing the achievement of Black charter-school students in comparison to Black public traditional school students is inconclusive. Nonetheless, charter schools are widely perceived to be the solution to otherwise failing traditional public-school systems (Almond 2012).

Critics argue that charter schools extract both students and necessary resources from local, traditional public schools and further complicate the Black-White achievement gap (Clark et al. 2015). Anderson (2016) discusses the recent phenomenon of charter schools as reflective of an ideological shift in the American ethos as it concerns education. Herein, Anderson contends that charter schools are driven by a businesslike model of free-market competition, whereby schools must contend with one another for consumers and market-enhanced education as the product that said consumers are buying into. Charter schools, by nature, embrace and promote a privatized, consumer logic. The charter-school model has resulted in a shift from a collective-based approach to education as a public good to that of an individualistic, consumeristic approach. The individualistic approach negates the notion that educational successes and failures translate into societal losses and gains; this inherently undermines a collective investment and reduces education to a product for consumption by the individual rather than the community (Anderson 2016). The commodification of a public good such as education poses a very real threat to the most socioeconomically vulnerable of groups: Black children. Anderson encapsulates this sentiment in arguing,

> When schools are conceived of as businesses, what were once institutions aimed at promoting the lives of individuals in a democratic society—ideals reflected in some of the most monumental Supreme Court rulings of the past century—become a means for generating revenue for an elite (2016, 43).

Most alarming is the notion that the charter model problematizes the most vulnerable—low-income children, minoritized children, and differently abled children—as a costly threat to the profit margin (Anderson 2016). With themes of academic rigor trumpeted across charter schools, stricter policies are commonly enforced whereby students are more likely to be suspended or expelled; this is particularly true for Black students as they constitute the majority of students in charter schools and are most susceptible to racial biases. The charter-school business model further propels these harsh practices to maintain and increase academic results, in order to protect the very product that they are selling. Shedd (2015) argues that attempts to desegregate public schools, such as the school-choice programs, often leave parents out of options as familiar neighborhood schools close to their homes are closed or combined with other schools. School closures in urban districts due to underperformance and insufficient resources disproportionately affect African American and Latinx students belonging to low-income families (Kirshner et al. 2010). Critics argue that charter schools not only destabilize traditional public schooling but also counteract gains made in equality and civil rights in the last decade, thus, posing a greater threat to the Black-White achievement gap.

THE ABSENCE OF "CHOICE" IN "SCHOOL CHOICE"

While marketed as promising vehicles for desegregation within the education system, charter and magnet schools continue to institutionalize practices that further marginalize the most vulnerable by hindering accessibility while prioritizing the interests of Whites. These schools complicate the enrollment process for parents, requiring them to become more knowledgeable and savvier throughout. This, naturally, proves to be disadvantageous for parents unable to be as involved in the process for a range of reasons (Archbald 2004). In her work as director of Scholar Success at Hartford Youth Scholars—a local, nonprofit college-access organization located in Hartford, Connecticut—coauthor, Brittany Rodriguez, is tasked with guiding families through the various enrollment processes for Hartford Region School Choice Programs. These programs are implemented by the Greater Hartford Regional School Choice Office (GHRSCO)—established by the Connecticut State Department of Education (CSDE)—and aim to offer "a broad variety of school choice opportunities that empower families to choose opportunities for their students and to enable student success". Per RSCO, school-choice options consist of magnet schools, Connecticut technical high schools, and open-choice schools. In accordance with the aforementioned description of magnet schools, RSCO defines magnet schools as unique public schools that offer particular thematic or specialized instructional programming. Connecticut technical high-school system schools are described as combining core academics and career and technical education to prepare students for immediate employment, apprenticeship, college, and career opportunities (*GHRSCO and CSDE* n.d.).

Open choice is pitched as a model for Hartford-resident students to attend public schools in nearby suburban school districts. It is worth noting that RSCO employs the term "allows" in reference to Hartford students attending suburban school districts, which connotes an element of suburban superiority in comparison to Hartford's respective urban schools. In Rodriguez's professional experience, magnet school and open-choice programs prove to be the most complex of these three program offerings—magnet schools due to the high demand for seats, and open-choice due to zoning and transportation restrictions. RSCO attempts to break down the various facets of each program by providing a twenty-six-page reference guide, eleven pages of which are in English and the remainder in Spanish, containing important application deadlines, application requirements and procedures, zoning and transportation maps, and lists of qualifying schools (*GHRSCO and CSDE* n.d.). The sheer length of this reference guide is reflective of the many moving parts that parents or guardians are tasked with navigating to place their children in a school of their "choice."

Rodriguez finds even with reference guides and organized informational panels with RSCO professionals, many families continue to struggle in distinguishing between programs and are further deterred by the complex enrollment process. This, coupled with the notion that poorer non-White families have smaller social networks and accompanying resources, hinders families' capacity to make informed decisions in choosing the best educational route for their children and themselves. Even upon successful enrollment, accessibility to these schools is disputed and understood as serving in the interests of more privileged families while further ostracizing marginalized families. RSCO, for example, offers limited transportation for students attending magnet or open-choice schools dependent upon residential location, leaving many families to sort out their own transportation. This does not pose an issue for families with greater access to necessary resources, such as personal vehicles or familial support, whereas families without these luxuries are disadvantaged due to socioeconomic restraints that impede their child's academic experience. Not only this, but students of color who are forced to travel outside their neighborhoods to obtain quality education are seen as outsiders in their mostly White schools. Such students also experience heightened harassment from police and are more likely to notice and experience discrimination than their peers in mostly Black schools. Furthermore, administrative staff within RSCO experience significant turnover, further limiting family support as new staff are less privy to enrollment details and processes.

Family accessibility to RSCO staff also proves to be of concern. Rodriguez's staff, as representatives of an established partner organization within the Hartford community, have experienced significant delays in getting a hold of staff due to substantial turnover when coordinating informational sessions for local families regarding school-enrollment processes. To this end, Rodriguez argues that the "choice" in "school choice" is a relative determinant based on a given families' socioeconomic means, whereby the wealthier White students are at a greater advantage than their poorer non-White peers.

Critical Race Theory

As observed during the *Brown vs. Board of Education* case of 1954, we see resistance to a push for the decentralization of Whiteness in public-school curricula whereby more accurate conceptualizations of America's racially triggered history are not dulled, bypassed, ignored, or overlooked as it traditionally has been. Although Critical Race Theory (CRT) has been around since the 1970s, there has been a more visible push to incorporate it into school curricula nationwide over the last decade. Herein, there is a clear call for addressing racism and drawing connections to the larger social context within the education system (Parker 2003). CRT serves to decenter the prominence of class and socioeconomic status found in critical legal studies and posits race as the primary lens through which legislation and political enactments are viewed (Chapman 2007). Proponents of centering CRT in contemporary curricula argue that racism plays a critical role in everyday life and is deeply ingrained in the historical foundations of American civilization, which should not be overlooked any longer. More specifically, CRT declares that race plays a fundamental role in the evolution of nation-empire, the creation of capital, and the shaping of culture and identity (Parker 2003). Incorporating an accurate portrayal of African American history—which *is* American history, to be clear—has elicited pushback from opponents of CRT in what proves to be a power struggle across the Black-White binary. Republican officials reject CRT's approach to addressing race and racism as core features of U.S. history, laws, and institutions (Simon 2021). Julian Hayter, historian and professor at the University of Richmond, suggests that CRT is a scapegoat for political figures who are neither interested in reconciling nor teaching America's racial history in the classroom because, in doing so, such mandates a racial reckoning (Hayter cited in Simon 2021). Hayter points out that, while the present racial awakening is bringing forth the untold stories and events of Black history, the telling of American history for most of the 20th century has excluded certain peoples' history, particularly non-Whites'. There is underlying irony in how truly American it is to normalize the erasure of entire groups of peoples' histories; this is true for Indigenous groups, African Americans, Asians, and the list goes on. Simon (2021) makes the necessary distinction between heritage and history—whereby the former is a romanticized version of the past that omits the uglier parts and the latter an attempt to interpret actual events in accordance with rules of evidence—in an effort to draw attention to the fact that most Americans understand heritage but not quite history.

Herein lies the root problem: CRT requires that we overhaul American curricula to include American history as it has occurred, and not as received by students for centuries in altered, romanticized forms. Hayter contests opposing arguments that teaching CRT in the classroom would be harmful and unfair to White children considering these crimes were committed before their time by arguing that "recognition is restorative," that we can teach CRT without inflicting harm or guilt (Simon 2021). To this end, not only is it essential that we deconstruct norms around Whiteness and White privilege in the classroom and educational systems at large; it is doable through CRT. Teachers must be adequately trained in culturally responsive pedagogy and be able to demonstrate their ability to provide antiracist scholarship to all students. Public education as an institution does not function on its own as a source of oppression. When coupled with residential segregation and the disproportionate policing of Black children, the results are devastating.

Neighborhoods, Schooling, and Policing

Neighborhood residence undoubtedly affects schooling and educational attainment in a number of ways. Rothstein (2019) demonstrates this by way of making the connection between asthma rates among children belonging to low-income communities and residual challenges within respective classroom environments.

Due to poorly maintained housing and environmental factors, children in low-income communities are more likely to suffer from asthma. In fact, Black children residing in segregated, urban environments are four times as likely to have asthma in comparison to White children living in middle-class neighborhoods. Asthma has the potential to negatively impact a child's schooling experience in numerous ways, including hindering a child's ability to stay awake at school, remain focused, participate in physical activities, and even attend school. Additional environmental factors associated with negatively impacting the academic performance of children living in racially segregated communities include lead poisoning, stress, irregular sleep due to parents' work schedules/working multiple jobs, and general housing instability. Dually alarming, and in addition to negatively impacting the students' achievement gap, living in a segregated community can also lead to shorter life expectancies and higher rates of disease (Rothstein 2019). Finally, Black children learn at an early age that school is "not for them"—a narrative informed by how poorly they are treated by teachers, administrators, and SROs (Beger 2002).

The function of SROs is dictated by school policy that intentionally serves to police and control Black children. Alarmingly, over a thousand students across fourteen states within the United States are subjected to canine searches, a tactic that can be connected to slave patrolling practices (Beger 2002). Excessive funding is spent on in-school officers, and a growing concern is the lack of control school principals have over the officers working within the very schools they preside over. Beger (2002) contends that the ever-growing presence of officers in schools mirrors that of a prisonlike environment whereby the 14th Amendment rights of children are seemingly revoked. It is evident that Black children are overpoliced in the key environments responsible for shaping their self-identity, character, and their futures—namely their neighborhoods and primary schools. Consequently, Black children are often perceived as more dangerous than their White peers, even when they display the same behaviors (Maxime 2018).

Today, our schools are more segregated by race than at any time in the last forty years (Rothstein 2019). A result of neighborhood segregation is that public schools in the United States remain racially segregated even in today's post-*Brown v. Board of Education* era. Equally alarming is that due to limited interactions with or access to Black children outside poor, urban environments, SROs have deficit views of Black children (Maxime 2018). One of the most damaging and pernicious ways that school segregation affects Black children is through the school-to-prison pipeline.

The school-to-prison pipeline refers to the direct and indirect policies that function as conduits to the U.S. criminal justice system by targeting Black children as deviant or criminally inclined from a young age. Public schools in the United States marginalize and criminalize Black girls differently than Black boys, but the results are no less damaging (Morris 2012). Moreover, Black girls are more likely to be described as and reprimanded for being "unlady-like, loud, defiant, and precocious" than their White or Latina peers (Morris 2018, Nolan 2011). Because the lens through which Black girls are perceived is often through damaging stereotypes, they are regularly cast as deserving of the harm they receive. Furthermore, while Black girls only make up about 16 percent of the school population, one-third of all girls referred to law enforcement are Black girls and they comprise one-third of *all* female-based arrests (Civil Rights Data Collection 2020). Even more upsetting, some of the most alarmingly punitive actions have been directed at Black girls as young as six or seven (D'Arcy 2012).

Herein, it is not the behavior of Black children that results in suspensions per se; rather, it is perceptions of Black behavior, assumed criminality, and the level of "policing" of Black children by teachers and staff that are central contributing factors in suspension. The very nature of these policies reveals the extent to which intentional and systemic racism persists throughout the United States.

Following the Columbine school shooting of 1999, a number of policies were enacted in an effort to create a safer school environment. Several said policies were implemented that both directly and indirectly criminalize student behaviors and, not surprisingly, disproportionately affect Black students. Some of these federally enforced punitive school-discipline policies include "zero-tolerance policies," the Safe Schools Act, and the Gun-Free Schools Act. Zero-tolerance policies were initially created to prevent students from bringing weapons, namely guns, to school campuses. The Gun-Free Schools Act of 1994 requires any school that receives federal funding to expel any student that either brings or has determined to bring a firearm to school for at least one year.

In line with the broken-windows theory of criminality, these policies target young people engaging in minor infractions in hopes of preventing more serious behavior later on. While each state and school system varies in response to such infractions, behaviors that often warrant expulsion or arrest are identified as the following: bringing anything considered to be a weapon to school (this may include toy guns or swords), having any alcohol or drugs on campus (this can include tobacco, cigarettes, and over-the-counter drugs such as Tylenol or Midol); fighting (including minor verbal arguments), saying anything that could be perceived as a threat, and insubordination or any behavior considered to be disruptive (Maxime

2018). Interpretations of these behaviors are subjective, especially to the persons observing these behaviors, such as teachers and SROs. These policies are known to have a disproportionate effect on Black students and are often implemented with no regard for any supportive contextualization of the incident at hand, such as a student acting in self-defense.

While zero-tolerance policies purport to reduce any future negative behavior, school suspension and contact with the juvenile justice system at a young age actually *increases* the likelihood of contact with the criminal justice system later in life. Out-of-school suspensions disrupt students' learning progress. For example, the Center on Youth Justice at the Vera Institute of Justice found that "for similar students attending similar schools, a single suspension or expulsion doubles the risk that a student will repeat a grade" (Maxime 2018). And that "being retained a grade, especially while in middle or high school, is one of the strongest predictors of dropping out" (Shared Justice 2018). Early suspension is also a predictor of school dropout or failure to graduate on time (Maxime 2018). Sociologists argue that this is because students that have early experiences with being policed at a young age internalize punitive school-discipline policies and come to view schools as places of punishment rather than the safe institutions of learning and scholarship that they ought to be.

Again, these punitive school-discipline policies disproportionately affect Black students, and it has been found that levels of perceived "threat" are greater in schools where the student body is comprised of a larger percentage of non-White students (Welch and Payne 2010). These facts highlight the ways in which law enforcement policy, residential segregation, and school segregation intersect to negatively shape the experiences of Black children. Since the implementation of zero-tolerance policies, American public schools, particularly in urban areas, have adopted an increasingly punitive approach to student misbehavior despite decreases in crime rates, drug use, violent victimization, and delinquency since the 1990s (Beger 2002; Brooks, Schiraldi, and Ziedenberg 1999; Devoe et al. 2005; Dinkes, Cataldi, and Lin-Kelly 2007). Somewhat recent studies show that nearly all urban schools implement some form of surveillance that tracks the behaviors of students (Dinkes, Kemp, and Baum 2009), such as metal detectors, locked doors, gates, SROs, security cameras, drug-sniffing dogs, and locker searches (Beger 2002; Devoe et al. 2005; Giroux 2003; Hirschfield 2008; Watts and Erevelles 2004). These trends are not benign and not only affect the experiences of Black children at school but also, even more seriously, later on in life (Welch & Payne 2010). Students can be charged and convicted as adults yet are not given the same "rights" as adults. In the state of Connecticut alone, children as young as fourteen can be legally tried as adults and 97 percent of child inmates serving 50 years or more are Black or Latinx ("OLR Research Report" n.d.).

Neighborhood segregation clearly impacts those living in poor, segregated, urban environments in several ways. One of the most significant ways in which segregation impacts a person's life outcomes is how they are perceived and policed, even at young ages. The segregation of our neighborhoods and, consequently, our schools affects the ways Black youth are perceived by law enforcement, even when they themselves have never lived in a poor, urban environment. Whether or not Black students attend mostly White, selective-enrollment schools, Black students experience or witness police violence to a much greater extent than their White peers. These personal and vicarious experiences with law enforcement affect student views of justice and normalizes the punitive, "criminal gaze" through which they experience childhood. Due to a lack of regular contact in integrated settings with non-White people, White police officers and White community members perceive Black people as "not belonging" in White spaces and, thus, perceive them as threatening and act accordingly (Anderson 2012, 2016). This brings us to the nuances of policing Black people and the social construction of the "ghetto."

CHAPTER 6

Policing the Ghetto

> (The police) are a very real menace to every black cat alive in this country. And no matter how many people say, 'You're being paranoid when you talk about police brutality'—I know what I'm talking about. I survived those streets and those precinct basements and I know. And I'll tell you this—I know what it was like when I was really helpless, how many beatings I got. And I know what happens now because I'm not really helpless. But I know, too, that if he (police) don't know that this is Jimmy Baldwin and not just some other n***** he's gonna blow my head off just like he blows off everybody else's head. It could happen to my mother in the morning, to my sister, to my brother . . . For me this has always been a violent country—it has never been a democracy.
>
> —James Baldwin

While many are under the assumption that the 13th Amendment marked the end of slavery in the United States, in the eighty years between the Civil War and World War II Black laborers were forced to labor against their will. In other words, they were forced into involuntary servitude. Within this same timeframe, as many as eight hundred thousand people endured the South's corrupt system of justice. More than nine thousand prisoners died at the hands of the convict-leasing system within southern states and counties (Blackmon 2009). The 13th Amendment rendered little progress in the termination of systems of labor exploitation; rather, they changed shape and evolved.

The "end" of slavery resulted in the creation of several more systems of forced labor and terror for African Americans. Racial injustice took shape in the form of convict leasing, peonage, sharecropping, lynching, as well as the historic Jim Crow segregation. At this time, Black people were particularly vulnerable to being picked up, thrown in jail, and forgotten about in the system without reason; this, further demonstrating that Black people were barred from a fair justice system. Free Black people were vulnerable to being bought and sold to corporations and coal mines. Black people were brutalized and killed for no reason at all with little to no consequence to those committing these acts of violence. Not surprisingly, the federal government turned a blind eye to many of the forced laborers in the South and was complicit in forced labor. These newly created institutions had a direct impact on individual African Americans and had an indirect one on the entire African American population, each institution serving the common goal of eliciting terror, exploiting free labor, and maintaining a social hierarchy (Blackmon 2009).

Racism and the oppression of Black people within the United States was not by chance; rather, it developed from a series of very conscious decisions. The creation of a racial hierarchy, placing Whites as superior to all others, was enacted to profit White landowners and businessmen while also justifying their feelings of entitlement. Additionally detrimental to Black people was the widespread characterization of Black men as criminals, a narrative that was backed by intentional laws and policies serving to "criminalize Black life" and uphold the racial hierarchy. A system, or loophole, was developed allowing the continuation of forced Black labor by way of targeting and depicting Black men as criminals, even in cases that are not otherwise typically criminalized. Judges backed law enforcement officials who, then, cooperated with White business owners to generate a forced labor system that would profit wealthy White people upon the conviction and criminalization of Black men (Blackmon 2009).

Consider, now, how these systems of forced labor and systemic brutality have affected and continue to affect an entire group of people. Modern-day police brutality is yet another form of this same system of terror, evolved from the institution of slavery. Media outlets and social media feeds are inundated with photos, videos, audio, and writing that captures violence and injustice at the hands of law enforcement directed at Black people. Black people are at very real risk of being shot or killed for merely being in the presence of a police officer. Simple traffic stops take a turn for the worse and end in the shooting of a Black person, oftentimes without probable cause. Black people are being terrorized today through the same racially biased mechanisms that terrorized them throughout slavery and after the Civil War. Continuing to uphold policing, a system founded in slave patrolling, as it presently functions allows for the mechanisms that white supremacy depends on to thrive and persist in the brutalization of black people.

Characterizing Blackness

Early depictions of Black people during slavery, particularly men, characterized them as docile, happy, and content in their positions of inferiority in service to White people. Such depictions reflected an ability to control Black people and perpetuated the idea that slavery was the most fitting status for Black people. However, these depictions of docility shifted during Reconstruction as freed Black people began to challenge the foundations and institutions of White supremacy (Smiley and Fakunle 2016).

The characterization of Black men as subservient fools during slavery soon shifted to the portrayal of Black men as savage brutes and dangerous criminals—often characterized as directing their criminality and violence toward White women. As these myths of Black men grew, so did the practice of extrajudicial lynching as a means of striking fear throughout entire communities of Black people. When Black people were victims of extrajudicial crimes and violence at the hands of white people, rather than being characterized as victims, they were portrayed as violent monsters; thus, further perpetuating a deep fear of Black men within White communities (Smiley and Fakunle 2016; Litwack 2004). Several studies legitimize the notion that racial minorities are overrepresented as criminals and underrepresented as victims. Furthermore, even when young Black men are *victims* of police shootings, they are dehumanized, seen as superhuman, and criminalized (Dukes and Gaither 2017).

The racially driven, anti-Black characterization of Black people as inherently violent impacts the ways in which they are perceived by both the public and the police, and ultimately informs the level of accountability we hold the police to. Dukes and Gaither (2017) found that media depictions of Black victims directly shape public perception and levels of sympathy toward victims as sometimes deserving of the violence directed at them. When negative stereotypes were used to characterize the victims, the victims were seen as being more at fault for their own deaths than when positive stereotypes were used. Moreover, negative stereotyping of the victim resulted in less punitive measures and accountability for the shooters. Taking into consideration that negative stereotypes are more likely to be employed than positive ones with respect to Black men, the implications of this trend are far reaching and yield devastating results for Black communities. In a study of actual criminal cases, Goff et al. (2008) found that news articles about Black people contained more apelike imagery than articles about Whites. More importantly, those who were implicitly compared to apes were more likely to be executed than those who were not. Goff et al. argue that these dehumanizing depictions of Black criminals impact the ways in which they are treated and prosecuted by law enforcement. To this end, remnants of slavery, namely the justifications for inhumane treatment of enslaved people, that can also be found in modern-day depictions of Black victims as inhuman seemingly "justifies" their treatment by law enforcement.

The early criminalization of Black people has given way to a culture of fear around Blackness (Alexander 2010; Davis 1998; Muhammad 2010) and laid the groundwork for a ripple effect of politically backed initiatives at their expense. These initiatives include the War on Drugs, stricter sentencing guidelines, zero-tolerance drug policies, and disproportionate sentencing for Black crimes (Alexander 2010). This leads us to the current injustices of the mass incarceration of Black people that presently plagues our Black and minoritized communities.

ERASURE AND THE DEHUMANIZATION OF BLACK WOMEN

While not characterized as violent in the ways that Black men are, Black women continue to experience violence at the hands of police officers—incidents that too often go unnoticed or unmentioned. Black women regularly lose their lives to racially motivated violence—a reality that is absent from the national discourse around police and vigilante violence. One study found that in one jurisdiction in New York City rates of stops, frisks, and arrests were *identical* for Black men and women (ACLU of New York); however national discourse around the impact of policies such as stop and frisk only focus on how racial profiling affects Black men. While Black women are not portrayed as threatening in the same capacity that Black men are, internalizations of Black women as "superhuman" and not susceptible to pain affect how Black women are treated in encounters with police officers—these beliefs are amplified when Black women are poor, transgender, or gender-nonconforming (Singal 2014; Waytz, Hoffman, and Trawalter 2014; Brown and Klas 2014). This is compounded when Black women are experiencing mental health crises and turn to law enforcement for help. Rather than be treated with compassion, Black women are often criminalized in these moments and officers respond with deadly force (Blackwell 2014; Johnson and Gideon 2015; *Say Her Name: Resisting Police Brutality Against Black Women* 2015; Garrett 2015; Veklerov 2014; Meronek 2013; Pinto 2012; Rosenzweig 2002).

Black girls and women are exposed to violence at the hands of not only police but also one another and others in their own communities. Several scholars write about the experiences of Black men having to navigate the "code of the streets" (e.g., Anderson 1999), but they fail to acknowledge that Black girls must do the same. Jones (2009) argues that the violence that is localized in poor, segregated neighborhoods is not specific to boys and that girls must organize their lives around the same "three Rs" that boys do: reputation, respect, and retaliation. The erasure of these experiences and the violence girls must withstand often leaves them to grapple on their own with extreme inequality and sexism, as well as the criminalization and hypersexualization of their bodies.

Police Violence and Race

Police practices and tactics are overwhelmingly racially informed, as one can see through any examination of police policy. Upon examination of the data made available to the public, it can be ascertained that racial biases and practices on the part of police officers and departments yield grave implications for the Black community. Black men are far more susceptible to stops, searches, and arrests even when compared with White men engaging in the same behavior. Black men are, not surprisingly, policed far more heavily and harshly at each stage of the criminal justice process in comparison to Whites. Following suit, prosecutors charge Black men with more serious crimes at a much higher rate than Whites engaging in the same behavior. When reversed, criminal defendants are punished far less severely when the victim is Black (Davis 2017). African American men are twice as likely to be unarmed than Whites when killed by police (Alexander 2010), and while more White people are killed by police officers, African Americans are killed at a disproportionate rate. As a result, Black men comprise a disproportionate number of prisoners in jails across the nation (Davis 2017).

A recent *Newsweek* report shows that of misdemeanor arrests in 2014 alone, 86 percent of those arrested were people of color (Bekiempis 2014). Between 2002 and 2013, the NYPD issued more than six million summonses for "quality-of-life" violations, such as riding a bike on the sidewalk. Upon examination of 1.5 million of these summonses, 85 percent were issued to Black or Latinx people. This report also details that, when asked why minoritized comprise so many of these arrests, a spokesperson said that arrests are based on "officers' observation and criminal complaint." This proves troublesome as research reveals that officers hold more negative perceptions of Black and Brown people than of Whites. Black and Brown people are more likely to be perceived as engaging in criminal behavior than White people, thus increasing the likelihood that people will call the cops on them for low-level infractions. Unfortunately, due to federal laws regarding police reporting, very few data are available on how many people have actually been killed by police (Flatow 2014a). However, the data that are available reveal that Black teens were twenty-one times more likely to be killed by police than their White counterparts. These data are self-reported and departments are not legally required to submit information regarding number of shootings, and as such this number likely undercounts the number of actual shootings and deaths at the hands of officers. Further complicating this, shootings that were more overtly seen as unjustifiable are far less likely to be reported (Flatow 2014b). The NAACP presented statistics concerning forty-five officer-involved shootings in Oakland, California, that took place between 2004 and 2008. These statistics revealed that one-third of the shootings were fatal, and of the people that were shot, thirty-seven were Black, none were White and not one officer was charged (Bulwa 2010).

In 2007, *COLORLINES* and the *Chicago Reporter* conducted a national investigation of police shootings in America's ten largest cities. This investigation found that African Americans were overrepresented among police-shooting victims in all ten cities and both Black and Latinx people were overrepresented in numbers of people fatally shot by the police. In New York, Las Vegas, and San Diego, the percentage of Black people killed by police at least doubled their share of the city's total population of people shot by the police (Lowenstein 2007). Lee (2014), a former reporter for *Mother Jones*, argues simply that Black people are disproportionality represented among those targeted by officers. A 2013 *Gallup* survey reveals that within a thirty-day period, one in four African American males experience unfair treatment by police, which is significant considering most Americans have no interaction with police within that same time period (Newport 2013). By the end of 2009, the number of Black men in prison, jail, on probation, or on parole equaled approximately the same number enslaved in 1850—a fact that encourages serious contemplation and reassessment (Alexander 2010).

CRIME AND RACE

While the "War on Drugs" rose in popularity during the Reagan and Bush eras, it began in 1971 during the Nixon administration in an attempt to silence and disrupt the Black and antiwar activists of the 1960s and 1970s. Couched in language about concerns over safety for Americans, the Nixon administration directly targeted the Black population and made Black men America's public enemy number one. It was not only the White community that supported this characterization of Black male criminality, but the Black community as well. Black civil rights leaders called on the Black community to stand up against drug dealers so as not to diminish the gains of the civil rights movement. Of course, this perpetuated and exacerbated an already problematic view of the Black community—not limiting views of criminality to criminals but extending them to the entire Black population (Baum 1996). It wasn't until 2016 when John Ehrlichman, one of former President Nixon's top domestic policy aids, disclosed in an interview with Dan Baum that the connection between the drug war and anti-Black, antileftist ideology was clearly established.

> You want to know what this was really all about? The Nixon campaign in 1968, and the Nixon White House after that, had two enemies: the antiwar left and black people. You understand what I'm saying? We knew we couldn't make it illegal to be either against the war or black, but by getting the public to associate the hippies with marijuana and Blacks with heroin, and then criminalizing both heavily, we could disrupt those communities. We could arrest their leaders, raid their homes, break up their meetings, and vilify them night after night on the evening news. Did we know we were lying about the drugs? Of course we did (Baum 2016).

This mass characterization of criminality regarding the Black community, as well as an increasingly punitive response to drugs, led to the mass incarceration of Black people. Mass incarceration is defined as the rate of incarceration that is markedly above comparative and historical norms for liberal democracies (Western and Muller 2013). Furthermore, mass incarceration involves the extensive and concentrated imprisonment of not just the individual but the group. Between the years 1980 and 2000, the American prison population nearly quadrupled. This was not due to an actual net increase in crime, but rather the punitive drug policies enacted amid the War on Drugs campaign (Alexander 2010). Born out of this campaign, more stringent and far stiffer sentencing policies for drug crimes were enforced with tenacity, disproportionately affecting Black communities. Between 1993 and 2009, more people were incarcerated for drug crimes than for violent crimes, and while White people are more likely than Black and Latinx people to sell drugs, Black Americans are more likely to be incarcerated for drug-related offenses (Kendi 2019). Black and Latinx people remain overrepresented in the prison population despite their relatively lower levels in the U.S. adult population, and Black *nonviolent* drug offenders serve similar sentences to *violent* White criminals. Consequently, the intersectionality of racial and class-based inequalities produces the perfect storm for the penal confinement of Black men. The culmination of increased time served, increased prison admissions for drug crimes, as well as increased revocation of parolees contributed to our current system of mass incarceration, presently plaguing Black and Brown communities throughout the United States (Western and Muller 2013).

CRACK VS. HEROIN

The War on Drugs campaign brought forth a surge in media coverage related to crack use, particularly within poor Black and Brown communities. The Anti-Drug

Abuse Act of 1986 is a signature law of this era, which singles out crack offenders and extends the most severe punishment by mandating the same five-year minimum sentence for the possession of five grams of crack cocaine as five hundred grams of powder cocaine (Mullen et al. 2020). Despite the fact that most crack users were and still are White, Blacks were jailed at a disproportionate rate to that of Whites and faced far harsher punishment. Black drug offenders were punished far more severely than their white counterparts; Black drug offenders with little to no prior criminal history were sentenced to federal prison for an average of forty months longer than non-Hispanic Whites between 1991 and 2016. Blacks, too, were arrested far more frequently than their White counterparts—nearly two times as likely to be arrested. Furthermore, Blacks were overrepresented in media coverage and, thus, subjected to extensive scrutiny and judgment. This coverage further shaped the biases and narratives folks had about Black and Brown people as well as the conditions of their neighborhoods. This media push corroborated the further marginalization of Black people by positing them not only as dangerous criminals but also now as "crackheads" and "superpredators."

Despite the medical community knowing that drug addiction was a disease in the 1980s, political leaders opted not to treat the crack epidemic as a health issue; rather, it was treated as a criminal issue whereby addicts were arrested and jailed for their addiction. The crack epidemic, too, unveiled a racial double standard within the criminal justice system whereby Whites suffering from addiction were treated with compassion and humanity, whiles Blacks were jailed with little regard. This is evident upon closer examination of the current opioid epidemic, whereby the media urges empathy and health-care treatment for opioid addiction as this epidemic has taken root in affluent middle-class subdivisions. While one-fourth of the $1.7 billion of federal funds was provided to combat the crack epidemic with treatment and rehabilitation, nearly three-quarters of the $7.4 billion Congress has allotted in response to the ongoing opioid epidemic is earmarked for treatment and prevention programs. Public perception is not that of hostility or blame as was the case with the crack epidemic; rather, there has been a clear change in the language and overall approach whereby addicts are considered "victims" with consideration for the fact that this impacts the White community more intensely (Mullen et al. 2020). This is a stark contrast to the crack epidemic, whereby Blacks were charged, jailed, and, often, entrapped in the criminal justice wheelhouse with little to no empathy by the media, the general public, or the courts.

THE ROLE OF IMPLICIT BIAS

Elijah Anderson (2012) documents that perceptions of Blackness and the "ghetto" are not constrained by the physical boundaries of the proclaimed ghetto itself. Perceptions of Black people as representing the iconic nature of the "ghetto" far extend the physical boundaries of poor, segregated Black neighborhoods, which certainly has implications for the ways in which Black and Brown people are treated by law enforcement (Anderson 2012). Over the last several decades, social scientists have documented known biases among police officers against Black people (Eberhardt et al. 2004). Several studies have found that unconscious racial bias results in negative race-based behavior, activated by the prevalence of racial stereotypes linking criminality to race. Scholars have found that these biases against Black people, and Black men in particular, exist even among those who do not hold explicitly or consciously racist ideas about Black people. Implicit biases against racial minorities influence interaction with others, how actions are interpreted, when a gun is used, and they yield real-world consequences more generally (Kang 2005). Systematic racial biases in officer shootings are not so much informed by an expressed endorsement of racial stereotypes or feelings toward Blacks, as by knowledge of cultural stereotypes (Lane et al. 2007). These biases influence perceptions of whether someone is holding a weapon (Allport and Postman 1947), whether someone is perceived as being aggressive or dangerous (Devine 1989), and the probability and speed with which someone will decide someone is a perceived aggressor (Correll et al. 2002). Moreover, those with stronger perceptions of African Americans as hostile were more likely to shoot an unarmed Black suspect and less likely to shoot an armed White suspect (Lane et al. 2007). Eberhardt et al. (2004) find that there is significant correlation between race and perceived threat, in which subjects who simply looked at a Black face were more likely to see weapons regardless of the persons prejudice level. People were also more likely to shoot Black men with guns than White men with guns, and to shoot Black men without guns if there was any doubt over whether a gun was present or not. Eberhardt and others (2004) also found that when asking police officers, "Who looks like a criminal?" they chose more Black than White faces. In 2011, the NYPD made more stops of young African American men than there are young Black men in all of New York City (Flatow 2013). Racial bias is baked into every level of law enforcement, and implicit biases play out in the courtroom, in decisions or actions of prosecutors, jurors, Supreme Court justices, and others responsible for upholding justice fairly (Lane et al. 2007).

The mere *presence* of a Black man can signal thoughts of criminal behavior or intent regardless of the actions of the Black person (Eberhardt et al. 2004). In fact, just thinking about a Black person can trigger thoughts of aggression. Presumed racial biases yield potentially lethal consequences by enforcing narratives that simply being Black equates "lawlessness" and being Latinx indicates "criminality" (Goldberg 2015). This narrative has been posited as a throwback sentiment to the past whereby the first body, "the Black body" is lathered in racist projections and the actual individual at hand, considered "the second body," is forced to endure this violence. Moreover, the Black body is a site for remembered experiences that unfold the meeting point between the legal and extralegal in the present. The Black body occupies the intermediary space between slave and citizen, whereby the Black body is situated both within and outside the "national body"; the Black body is, then, simultaneously antimodern and modern (Goldberg 2015). It can be argued that the very policing of Black bodies, and racism more generally, is embedded in patriotism as normalizing violence against Blacks as well as control over their bodies transcends time and is embedded in the foundations of policing.

Well-established biases against African Americans do not stop at police interaction. Media, civilians, and government officials share the perception of young Black men as dangerous. For example, when comparing arrest rates with news coverage of Black men as perpetrators of violent crime, they are overrepresented in terms of news coverage but underrepresented in sympathetic, relatable roles (Entman and Gross 2008). This negative characterization in the media ultimately promotes public hostility toward Black and Brown victims (Dukes and Gaither 2017). Smiley and Fakunle (2016) found that, rather than characterizing victims in a sympathetic manner, the media tends to focus on their past or current criminal behavior, their physical stature (largeness) and clothing, the area of the incident as crime-ridden, and negative stereotypical elements of the victims' lifestyle. In some ways, these men are portrayed as criminals and thugs as a means of justifying the actions taken against them by law enforcement. Kang (2005) contends that news broadcasts of crimes function as "Trojan Horse viruses" that only increase implicit biases against minoritized people. Implicit bias shows up in how Black people are treated when trying to access housing and quality education as well. This results in real estate agents, lenders, and White neighbors making decisions that can make it impossible for Black people to access quality housing in affluent neighborhoods. Additionally, as housing inequality limits Black people's access to residential opportunity, it simultaneously limits their access to quality schools by way of residential segregation, home ownership, and property taxes. Moreover, as many White teachers have deficit views of Black communities in general, implicit bias shows up in how they educate children of color, how they treat them in the classroom, and whether they end up on the track to college or the track to prison.

BROKEN-WINDOWS POLICING

As mentioned in earlier chapters, broken-windows theory contends that visible signs of disorder demonstrate a lack of neighborhood concern and vigilance in which criminals identify as prime locations to commit serious crimes (Thompson 2015). As such, as means of preventing said crimes, law enforcement efforts are primed for the prevention of minor offenses that result in the appearance of disorder. However, broken-windows policing focuses on low-level infractions, disproportionately affects communities of color, and affects their relationships with and perceptions of law enforcement. Additionally, this type of policing impacts the ways in which law enforcement treat people of color; a graphic example being the killing of Eric Garner on July 17, 2014.

Among those disproportionately affected by broken-windows policing are Black women—especially poor or unhoused Black women, as these policies continue to criminalize poverty and uphold White middle-class interests (Kelling and Wilson 1982; Harcourt 2009; McCardle and Erzen 2001). When poverty is criminalized and coupled with deficit views of Black women, this results in the dehumanization of poor Black women, making it easier for officers to justify excessive force.

ACCOUNTABILITY FOR POLICE

The American justice system protects police through a number of laws and policing policies. The criminal justice system has implemented practices and laws that serve to protect law enforcement officers, perhaps most significant among these protections is qualified immunity. Qualified immunity is an affirmative defense that protects federal, state, and local officials that are sued for damages upon another person as long as their actions do not violate clearly established constitutional rights. Officials, including government employers, law enforcement officers, prison and jail guards, schoolteachers, school administrators, social workers, and more are protected by qualified immunity. Plaintiffs who sue such officials must demonstrate that the accused official's conduct violated "clearly established," constitutional rights of which reasonable persons would have known. Qualified immunity provides broad protection and has deterred an exorbitant amount of cases from reaching justice, as it proves to be one of the most impenetrable barriers to liability (Chen 2015). This means that even in cases in which police officers are in the wrong, they are unlikely to be held accountable for their actions (Flatow 2014b). The courts justify this type of legal immunity on several policy grounds, including claims that lawsuits against public officials performing their discretionary duties are often unfair seeing as they are not lawyers. Another of such grounds asserts that civil rights lawsuits may lead officials to be "over-deterred" in fulfilling their duties. A more recent argument points to the financial and social costs that such lawsuits bare. However, all too often individuals whose rights have been violated by officials are refused justice on the mere premise of qualified immunity, which, again, is applied very broadly. Critics of qualified immunity argue that the courts dismiss constitutional rights claims without, first, determining whether the official's conduct violated the constitution and, therefore, unjustly toss a potentially relevant case (Chen 2015). The "clearly established" clause in qualified immunity leads to the dismissal of many cases on the premise that misconduct cannot be clearly established, foregoing the constitutional matter at hand entirely (Pfander 2011). Federal prosecution of deadly or excessive force is scarce because prosecution has to prove "specific intent" for civil rights investigations, and it is rare that misconduct cases ever end up holding the officer accountable. In New York City, between 1977 and 1995, not a single officer was convicted of homicide for on-the-job shootings, despite many fatal shootings (Flatow 2014b). While this is but one example in New York City, we must emphasize that these practices are widespread in cities throughout the country. Racial disparities in policing and excessive force prove to be a persistent national problem. Each violent act against a Black person or killing of a Black person at the hands of law enforcement only serves as further verification that the system of law is premised on the very violence that it claims to serve in prevention of (Goldberg 2015).

STOP AND FRISK

The racial disparities found in the stop-and-frisk policy within the state of New York have been widespread. This practice has received public opposition on the basis of racial profiling and has been challenged in court on such basis multiple times (Coviello and Persico 2015). Advocates of this policy argue that by enforcing weapon and drug possession laws, more serious crimes may be prevented; this line of thought is similar to that of the broken-windows theory. Those in opposition, however, argue that racial biases on the part of police officers ultimately inform their decision as to who gets stopped and frisked and operates in violation of two constitutional protections, the fourth and fourteenth amendments (Goel et al. 2016). Police stops increased from 160,851 in 2003 to 685,724 in 2011 (Mearest 2015). While relatively demeaning for those stopped and frisked, it is particularly unnerving that this practice disproportionately targets minoritized people whom, as a result, become entangled in the criminal justice system (Coviello and Persico 2015). More than 80 percent of individuals stopped are Black or Hispanic (Goel et al. 2016). Goel et al. suggest that the stop-and-frisk policy may be unlawful in that the stop-and-frisk policy does not occur consistently under the premise of "probable cause"; racial bias influences and helps to inform who is stopped and frisked based on race. Goldberg (2015) addresses an added element of verbal abuse of power on the part of officers themselves when stopping potential suspects. Goldberg offers a glimpse into the normalization of practices whereby officers break codes of conduct, employ racialized and hierarchal language when handling a potential suspect, fail to name cause for stop or arrest, and abuse power by foregoing citizens' rights when stopping and frisking. The stop-and-frisk policy is a practice enforced by police officers serving as, at its core, yet another form of policing the bodies and movements of Black people, which is in direct correlation with the purpose of slave patrols as discussed in chapter 2. Thus, further demonstrating that contemporary policing continues to serve as a means for controlling and oppressing the Black population with consideration for the fact that policies and practices, such as stop-and-frisk, disproportionately impact and target Blacks as well as other racial minorities.

Segregation, Blackness, and Police Violence

Not one policy or action led to the culture of fear around Blackness to thrive. However, when residential segregation exacerbates stereotypes about Black people, Black neighborhoods, and Black criminality, we are left with a culture in which Black individuals are constantly policed, treated more harshly by our criminal justice system at every stage, and are regularly characterized as "deserving" when they are victims of police violence. If the United States is to undo the impact of violent policing on Black people in America, we must focus our efforts on undoing the systemic impact of how Black children and Black adults are characterized as violent in American communities and schools. As much as we must work to desegregate our schools and our communities, we must also work to undo the ways in which the United States has characterized Blackness as superhuman, criminal, or invisible. A first step is to invest in Black communities while we disinvest in policing—this includes removing School Resource Officers from public institutions of learning.

Defunding the police and reinvesting in communities involves municipalities reallocating significantly more money that would typically go into policing every year to community resources such as education, housing, and mental health clinics. For example, investing in school nurses and social workers rather than SROs to work with children who are struggling, is one way in which we can shift from punitive reactions to students to more compassionate ones. Similarly, investing in affordable or free mental health programs, pathways to jobs, and access to affordable, mixed-income housing can provide people with the resources they need, which is much more of a deterrent to crime than policing is. We will discuss the divestment movement more extensively in chapter eight.

CHAPTER 7

The Contemporary Police State

> A system that perpetually condones the killing of people, without consequence, doesn't need to be revised, it needs to be dismantled!
>
> —Colin Kaepernick

Despite modern-day American policing and cultural traditions originating in England, police in England rarely use force. Why, then, is brutal—often deadly—force at the hands of police so shamefully common in America? When it comes to police killings, the United States remains appallingly unmatched in comparison to other industrialized nations (Hirschfield 2015). Police violence within the United States is disturbingly common and is woven into the very fabric of American life, particularly for Black people. This becomes evident upon closer examination of the origins of policing and the ways in which racialized practices have evolved over time and continue to manifest themselves in contemporary policing. The state of contemporary policing is particularly devastating to Black communities due to the onset of military-influenced practices that have become both institutionalized and commodified within the United States. The militarization of policing, the War on Drugs, and American gun culture converge with racial-residential segregation to produce life-threatening socioeconomic disadvantages for Black people.

The War on Drugs

Former U.S. President Richard Nixon successfully leveraged ratings and seized the 1968 election by positing a "war on drugs" as the epicenter of an envisioned response to modern crime issues. Nixon's presidency is undoubtedly marked by his law-and-order crusade and War on Drugs campaign, which set the precedence for his time in office and modern policing to come. Radley Balko (2014) contends that despite Nixon's plans for the "tough on crime" approach to serve more as a symbolic platform, it quickly cemented crime policy and laid the foundation for the type of policing we observe today. The explosion of military techniques by law enforcement officers and local units, coupled with the centralization of crime control as a means of addressing social issues, has given way to a prison-industrial complex unlike in any other country. The U.S. prison population has increased tenfold since 1970, a trend resulting from the War on Drugs and accompanying criminal justice policies enforced under Nixon's political agenda. This upward trend is not in response to growing crime rates nor any data supporting the efficacy of harsher policies, but rather to benefit a political agenda and capitalize on newfound sources of profit (Heitzeg 2014).

The Nixon administration viewed drug crime as the common denominator among low-income Black people, the counterculture, and the ongoing antiwar movement, which Nixon's unified Whites rallied against. No-knock warrants, preventive detention, and loose search warrants were proposed by the Nixon administration and, most irresponsibly, little discussion was had about the constitutionality of these policies nor their projected impact on the communities they were enforced in—predominately poor Black communities. Instead, Nixon and his administration moved forward with declaring drugs a national threat, setting the tone for the aggressive federal drug fight to come. Nixon preyed on, and amplified, racial stereotypes in describing drug users and dealers as inhumane while spewing dehumanizing rhetoric used to posit those participating in the drug trade as a national threat (Balko 2014). Not surprisingly, framing crime, terrorism, and drug-related issues with militaristic language has resulted in actions framed by a military paradigm (Kraska 2001).

THE MEDIA

The media played a vital role in the success of Nixon's War on Drugs crusade by corroborating his campaign and shaping public opinion through racialized narratives aimed at depicting predominately Black and Brown groups in association with drug use, distribution, and sale. The message here was that Black people are inherently responsible for America's "drug problem" (Sirin 2011). Television shapes which issues we think about and how we think about them, in part because television consumption is so readily available in the average home. To the detriment of Black communities, news coverage does not paint an accurate picture of crime in America. It is of no surprise that Black and Latinx people are overrepresented as offenders and underrepresented as victims, while crimes involving White victims are overreported (Heitzeg 2014). This is a vital point of contention in discussion of the War on Drugs' role in today's state of mass incarceration. The country's long-standing history of portraying Black people as criminals made them easy targets during the War on Drugs and continues to impact how they are treated within the American criminal justice system. Media perpetuates criminalized views of racial and ethnic minorities, furthering the racial agenda of America's War on Drugs by reinforcing exclusionary practices and policies that target such groups (Sirin 2011). For example, media depictions of criminal activities on the part of African Americans are more likely to emphasize violence and drug crimes, highlight racial and ethnic differences between offender and victim, and portray African Americans in police custody especially via the mug shot. Sirin points out that the overrepresentation of Black people in criminal activities, particularly with respect to drug dealing, is less reflective of their actual participation and more a reflection of selective law enforcement. Moreover, an officer operates not in response to an individual's actions per se, but rather in response to their own assumptions rooted in racially ascriptive reasoning. Sirin concludes that racial profiling is, in fact, quite closely tied to the Drug Enforcement Agency, otherwise known as the DEA. The DEA quite literally incorporated racial profiling tactics into the training of roughly twenty-seven thousand local and state law enforcement officers nationwide. Racial profiling creates an environment in which those who fit criminal profiles are often innocent, while those who do not fit the profile fail to even appear on law enforcement's radar and evade the system all together. Defenders of racial profiling as a tool argue that racial disparities in rates of arrest and conviction for drug crimes correspond with racial differences in criminal behaviors. However, we know this to not be true. The discretionary nature of drug law enforcement allows for racialized investigations that lead to racially biased arrests and convictions. Sirin argues that if a state aims to crack down on a particular crime by targeting communities of color, the statistics will distort the nature and scope of the problem at hand because they are not representative of all racial groups. This proved to be the case with Nixon's war on drugs, despite that numerous studies have shown no ascribed link between race or ethnicity and the likelihood to engage in criminal activity, including drug crimes.

FAR FROM OVER

Nixon started a "war" that proves to be far from over, a war that persists to the detriment of Black communities in pursuit of expanding the prison-industrial complex. The term "prison-industrial complex" refers to a self-perpetuating machine in which a convergence of special interests—including private companies and politicians who exploit crime to benefit their own agendas—profit under the premise that mass incarceration is a viable solution to socioeconomic issues (Heitzeg 2014). Despite the overall ineffectiveness of Nixon's war on drugs in terms of lowering crime and the drug trade, billions of dollars have been directed to its efforts (Sirin 2011). The War on Drugs has, however, been effective in exacerbating racial injustices through punitive policies that further deepen disparities presently plaguing Black communities—proving to be a war on racially marginalized groups. We see this manifest itself in the disproportionate number of Black people that make up the growing prison population within the United States. The number of people incarcerated for drug offenses increased from roughly forty thousand in 1980 to half a million in 2009. The total number of those incarcerated for drug offenses in 2009 is greater than the total number of people incarcerated for *all* offenses in 1980. In 2009, African Americans and Latinx people constituted roughly two-thirds of people incarcerated for drug offenses in state prisons, even though most crack cocaine users are White Americans (Sirin 2011; Provine 2007).

It is important to look closely at how drug abuse is perceived in affluent, White communities as compared with less affluent non-White communities. More affluent, predominantly White communities tackle drug use as a family or health problem, whereas drug use in less affluent communities is treated as a criminal problem that requires aggressive law enforcement. The mass incarceration of Black people, and other racially marginalized groups, is the byproduct of systems that work to criminalize groups of people based on intimately racialized policies and policing tactics for political gain and profit. Incarceration directly impacts the very communities that Black people are yanked from. Children belonging to such communities, for example, are further deprived of potential social capital with each jailed community member, further confining them to racially segregated communities.

To be clear, racial-residential segregation is not only harmful because it separates people based on skin color, but also because it blocks access to vital resources that would otherwise offer upward socioeconomic mobility. For example, residential segregation prevents Black people and other racially marginalized groups from accessing quality schools, mentorship programs, health care, mental health resources, extracurricular activities, and affordable nutritious food. Racial-residential segregation is at the heart of issues presently acting as socioeconomic barriers for many Black children and families. As such, we must critically analyze and address contributing factors to the systemic issue at large, including the War on Drugs and its lasting influence on Black communities.

The Militarization of Contemporary Policing

The militarization of policing within the United States has reshaped what police engagement looks like at the ground level. To effectively address this, we must, first, clearly define what militarism and militarization mean. *Militarism* is "a set of beliefs, values, and assumptions that stress the use of force and threat of violence as the most appropriate and efficacious means to solve problems." *Militarization* is "the implementation of the ideology of militarism. It is the process of arming, organizing, planning, training for, threatening, and sometimes implementing violent conflict." Police militarization is the process in which civilian police implement and arrange themselves around the tenets of militarism (Kraska 2007).

The dismantling of the 1878 Posse Comitatus Act, prohibiting military involvement in internal security or police matters except under the most extreme circumstances, has given way to an unprecedented level of military participation in internal-security matters. Four dimensions of the military model have been identified to provide tangible evidence of the militarization of the police force: (1) material—martial weaponry, equipment, and advanced technology; (2) martial language, appearance, beliefs, and values; (3) the organizational—martial arrangements such as "command and control" centers, elite squads of officers mirrored after military special operations patrolling high-crime areas; and (4) the operational—patterns of activity modeled after the military, especially in the areas of intelligence, supervision, the handling of high-risk situations, and war-making/restoration (Kraska 2007). The growing relationship between U.S. military and U.S. civilian police has led to the shift in the very policing we see daily. One such example is the notable growth and normalization of police special-operations units (SWAT teams), which are modeled after elite military special-operations units.

Daryl Gates is attributed with having started America's first SWAT team in the late 1960s. Balko (2014) argues that the birth of Gates's SWAT team changed the face, landscape, and culture of policing within the United States for generations to come. A number of events contributed to the formation of America's first SWAT team during the late 1960s, including the Watts riots, Whitman's 1966 massacre, and the Delano Grape Strike. It was around this time that Gates began consulting with marines, including Jeff Rogers who went on to lead America's first SWAT team, to develop what is now employed in major cities across the nation. Although Gates faced initial opposition from superiors who were not fond of his quasi-militaristic operation, he gradually gained political support and was greenlighted to explore a more militaristic approach to contemporary policing. A 1969 Gallup poll titled "The Troubled American: A Special Report on the White Majority" demonstrates that Whites were in favor of Gates's more aggressive approach to policing at the time. Results show that 85 percent of Whites believed that Black militants were let off too easily, 65 percent believed unemployed Black people were more likely to receive government aid as compared with their White counterparts, and 66 percent believed that police needed to be given more power. This poll offers contextualization as to the perceptions of White Americans at the time of Gates's push for a more militarized police force.

America's first SWAT raid took place in 1969 at the headquarters of the Black Panthers located in Los Angeles, and was considered an absolute tactical disaster. The Black Panthers served as a scapegoat for White Americans to further perpetuate racial stereotypes and push the narrative that Black people are a threat to the nation. This, too, benefited Nixon's agenda with respect to rallying Whites in his favor and garnering their support. Regardless of its ineffectiveness, Balko (2014) asserts that the most important element of the militaristic movement was public relations and, as such, the first raid was considered a great success despite its tactical shortcomings. During this raid, Gates received permission from the Department of Defense—whose mission statement reads, "Our mission is to provide the military forces needed to deter war and ensure our nation's security"—to use a grenade launcher against the Black Panthers, which suggests that this group was considered a threat to national security (Balko 2014; U.S. Dept of Defense n.d.). This action also speaks to the growing relationship between U.S. policing and the government military, further closing the gap between civil action and use of military equipment. While this first raid is an important historical reference, the nationally televised shootout of 1973 involving a terrorist group referred to as the Symbionese Liberation Army (SLA) in Los Angeles is responsible for making SWAT a household name. The term *SWAT teams* went on to trend in pop culture and was featured in television drama, board games, action figures, and other marketable items that only further solidified its place in American policing and popular consciousness. Police militarization exploded in the 2000s with new lucrative sources of funding and equipment resources, namely homeland security. The 20th-century trend of paramilitary practices as a means of making a political statement continued well into the 21st century, particularly in response to political protests. The terrorist attack of September 11, 2001, further exasperated these efforts and opened the floodgates for increased militarization funding under the guise of terrorism prevention. SWAT teams were more readily employed and utilized for more mundane crimes as they became increasingly appealing to civilian police (Balko 2014; Kraska 2007). U.S. police agencies have come to rely on the military model for a growing range of tasks and the Pentagon has given away millions in military equipment pieces such as grenade launchers to police departments for everyday use. There was an increase in the total number of police paramilitary deployments or callouts of 1,400 percent between 1980 and 2000 alone. In 2007, an estimated forty-five thousand SWAT team deployments were conducted, compared with an average of about three thousand in the early 1980s. This uptick is associated with the War on Drugs during the late 1980s through the 1990s when more than 80 percent of these deployments were in response to drug raids in which no-knock entries were executed in search of contraband (Kraska 2007).

This type of policing yields fatal results, particularly for Black people and other racially marginalized groups. The militarization of police has invoked an "us versus them" culture in which law enforcement and civilians are positioned on opposite teams. Law enforcement is not considered an entity tasked with protecting and serving its civilians, wherein cops are simply everyday civilians that share a connection with their community. A cultural dynamic has formed in which civilians, especially Black folks, do not look to officers for protection. Instead, marginalized communities seek protection from the police. Police approach civilians as the enemy, rather than valued members of a shared community. Lartey (2015) found that U.S. police killed more people in the first 24 days of 2015 than British and Welsh police have killed in the last 24 years. In fact, the United States is the only country in the Western world that has daily police killings (Baird 2015). Over six hundred thousand police officers patrol the streets of American cities every day, and each day roughly two or three officers kill someone (Hirschfield 2015). Langton and Durose (2013) found that in 2011, over a hundred and fifty thousand Americans reported the use of "excessive force" during their most recent traffic stop.

The courts have bent to allow officers more freedom and protection with each coming year. For example, the courts have exempted officers from the knock-and-announce requirement if they believe it would result in the suspect destroying evidence (Balko 2014). This no-knock bill was passed with great enthusiasm from the New York assembly and state senate. A no-knock raid is most commonly employed in search of contraband within private residences. During these raids, police are equipped with military gear and employ military-influenced tactics. Civilians are attacked at predawn hours, and police are dressed in all black and armed with military helmets, rams, and entry explosives (Kraska 2007). Not only does this create a highly volatile situation for all parties, but it is further complicated by the fact that police need only testify that there was reason to believe announced entrance would lead to the disposal of evidence (Balko 2014). If citizens are not immediately compliant, both nonlethal and lethal force are often employed (Kraska 2007). This, too, yields very real repercussions upon examination of the growing number of "wrong-door" and "botched" raids, whereby innocent citizens have been victim to unannounced police intrusions in which they are understandably subjected to terror, shock, and occasionally mistakenly killed (Balko 2014; Kraska 2007). For example, seven-year-old Aiyana Mo'nay Stanley-Jones was tragically killed during a police raid when officers, at the wrong apartment, shot a single bullet into her home as she was asleep on the couch next to her grandmother (Leduff 2010). The Breonna Taylor case of 2020 is, again, a perfect example of the dangers that unannounced intrusions, such as night raids, yield. Breonna Taylor's partner mistakenly shot at officers who unexpectedly, and unannounced, invaded their home in the dead of night. Although Taylor's partner responded to presumed trespassers out of self-defense, self-defense claims are generally unsuccessful in these cases. Taylor's partner, Kenneth Walker, was charged with attempted murder after shooting and injuring a police officer when the officers who killed Taylor entered the home unannounced. Walker's charges were eventually dropped in March 2021 but the officers who killed Taylor have still not been charged with any crimes. Another example of the freedoms afforded to officers is stop-and-frisk policy, whereby they are allowed to stop, frisk, and detain any person based on nothing more than a "reasonable suspicion." Again, this approach is testimonial-based and near impossible to measure or benchmark (Balko 2014).

Kraska (2007) argues that the inability of a government to clearly distinguish between the military and the police is a clear indicator of a repressive state and marks the decline of democracy. The traditional distinctions between military and police, war and law enforcement, and external and internal security are increasingly blurred. As a result, the U.S. military is observed to operate more as a police force—exemplified by the postinvasion conflicts in Iraq and Afghanistan—and vice versa as American police forces continue to take on a more militaristic approach to civilian policing. The rapid acceleration of the U.S. military into law enforcement operations post-9/11 has required a significant collaboration between civilian police, armed forces, and the military. The result of this trend is progressively skewed roles and perceptions between civilian policing and the military whereby Black communities suffer the brunt of consequences, often paying with their lives.

THE HERO COP

Robin G. Steinberg (2015) argues that the United States as a nation will never be able to substantially advance the causes of social and racial justice until we, first, challenge and effectively unravel the false narrative of heroic police officers engaging in dangerous war against its own citizenry, particularly Black men. The hero-cop narrative is built on a nationalistic appreciation for those who protect and serve the United States and instills an "us versus them" mentality that positions law enforcement against Black men. Arguably more than any other group, police have managed to portray themselves as indispensable heroes engaged in life-threatening war, despite the reality that, while there are real harms in that line of work, the true harm stems from the proliferation of this very narrative. This narrative makes it nearly impossible to question, challenge, or counter police objectives and action. Moreover, it is increasingly difficult to effectively address the near total absence of accountability of law enforcement without being the recipient of significant pushback and demonization. More devastating is the notion that the hero-cop narrative perpetuates imbalances within the criminal justice system whereby the system favors police over its own citizens. Antipolice rhetoric on the part of professionals working within or for the criminal justice system is not only taboo but interpreted as synonymous with being in favor of killing cops. Steinberg asserts that this is rooted in America's deep-seated perception that all parties belonging to the system are bound together as a part of a larger entity and, as such, are bound to an objective, idealized notion of justice, sharing a common goal, regardless of individual roles. To challenge the hero-cop narrative is an effort to do away with the portrayal of all law enforcement as inherently good, because the reality is that this is simply untrue and, ultimately, works to displace accountability. Instead, Steinberg contends that we must make policies that curb law enforcement's excesses and recognize that society's treatment of marginalized racial groups, particularly Black people, goes beyond any individual law enforcement officer or agent. Steinberg describes the criminal justice system as a processing plant designed to funnel poor people, particularly people of color, into the systems of jail, prison, probation, parole, bail, fines, and fees, which commandeer what little socioeconomic independence they have. Steinberg suggests that the persistent tensions that exist between the police and the policed may only be narrowed, first, with the permanent ending of oppressive police tactics such as broken-windows policing, the normalizing of police accountability, and the demilitarizing of the police force.

Gun Culture in the United States

Rising demand for increased production of firearms during the Civil War due to the growing need for arms and a desire to provide one gun each to the majority of soldiers perpetuated a culture of arms that continued into the mid-20th century and gave birth to what we know as American gun culture. Bellesiles (2002) contends that the role of firearms in American life began with the American Revolution. While guns are now considered a prominent fixture of American culture, this was not always the case and certainly not for Black people. In fact, the Second Amendment was designed to safeguard slaveholders' ability to control the Black population during slavery, and it was the responsibility of White men to extinguish slave rebellions by hunting down fugitive slaves and returning them to their owners. This relationship between White mens' "right to bear arms" and the need to "control" the movements of Black people is firmly intact today. We see this in cases of police brutality across the United States whereby officers shoot at Black people found legally carrying a weapon. For example, Alton Sterling, on July 5, 2016, in Baton Rouge, Louisiana (a right-to-carry state), was killed by law enforcement after they had mistaken him for another man who was allegedly threatening a convenience-store clerk. The very next day, Philando Castile was pulled over by police in St. Paul, Minnesota, after being mistaken for a robbery suspect. When reaching for his ID, Castile told officers that he had a gun and was permitted to carry a concealed weapon—this information propelled Officer Jeronimo Yanez to begin shooting Castile resulting in his death (Anderson 2021).

In stark contrast, we see time and again White men "defending" themselves and their property in instances where they can legally (and illegally) carry weapons and walk away unharmed by law enforcement. On January 2, 2016, Ammon Bundy and several other armed far-right extremists occupied the Malheur National Wildlife Refuge in Harney County, Oregon, with zero casualties (Berry 2016). It is relevant to note that before this event Bundy and roughly three hundred people gathered in a Safeway parking lot, and then marched outside the sheriff's office and the county courthouse without any police intervention (Peacher 2016; Wilson 2016). One would assume that the Bundy militia—later calling themselves the Citizens for Constitutional Freedom—of approximately 150 armed men would have been met with strong police presence upon seizing the Wildlife Refuge (House 2016). During the first few weeks of the invasion, militia members were allowed to come and go from the refuge without intervention from law enforcement. It wasn't until over a month later that the militia surrendered after mounting pressures from the FBI and local law enforcement. It is not hard to imagine what the outcome of this type of occupation would have been had the entire militia been armed Black men taking over federal land (Phipps and Levin 2016). More recently, on January 6, 2021, a mob of armed Donald Trump supporters stormed the U.S. Capitol in Washington, D.C., equipped with pipe bombs, Molotov cocktails, and automatic weapons. These domestic terrorists were able to occupy and vandalize the building for several hours before police successfully intervened (Luke 2021). Not only were the armed rioters encouraged by former president Donald Trump to storm the Capitol, the sparse presence of law enforcement and complete absence of the National Guard allowed them to do so. The absence of the National Guard is significant considering the overbearing presence of the National Guard at the peaceful Black Lives Matter protests during the summer of 2020 in the wake of the murders of George Floyd and Breonna Taylor. This is further complicated by an FBI investigation finding that Capitol police were forewarned well in advance that this insurgence was to take place—further demonstrating the implicit biases that plague contemporary policing.

Hirschfield (2015) identifies two related factors impacting U.S. policing as the focus on rugged individualism and self-reliance. A link between self-reliance and police killings is the gun culture that this climate reflects. Hirschfield finds that eight out of the ten states in his sample area are located in the Mountain or Western regions, where traditions of "rugged individualism" are far higher. Police in Western states within Hirschfield's sample exhibit killing rates nearly triple those in Northeastern states. Handguns, legal or otherwise, are easy to obtain and police never know if they will be encountering someone with a dangerous weapon. In gun culture, police are prepared for the possibility that a suspect may be armed. Thus, American police have killed people by mistakenly identifying a nonlethal object, such as a wallet or phone, as a gun. Because hesitation on the officer's part can yield fatal results, we have culturally and legally sanctioned the officer's use of force. Granting this leeway to often-nervous police can be dangerous as some may disguise malice for fear (Rothkopf 2015). American gun culture coupled with racism has severe implications for policing in America.

Race and Policing of Communities

Make no mistake, race is most certainly a central point of contention as it concerns violence and the excessive use of force by law enforcement. Police violence is a tool used to maintain racial segregation and inequality (Hirschfield 2015). Violence against racially marginalized groups is one area in which excessive use of force occurs that deserves attention, particularly with consideration for the fact that Black people are overrepresented among police victims (Baird 2015; Hirschfield 2015). Among victims of police killings in 2015, Black and Latinx people were twice as likely to be unarmed than Whites (Swaine et al. 2015). A consequence of racial profiling, accompanied by other racially driven practices, is the loss of confidence and trust on the part of Black communities with respect to the U.S. criminal justice system, and rightfully so. This loss of trust and confidence in police encourages social divisions as law enforcement drives tensions among racially marginalized groups and simultaneously feeds racially driven suspicion of groups—all resulting in public demand for stricter measures against marginalized groups (Sirin 2011) and further fueling an already racially focused system in which marginalized groups become entrapped in the criminal justice system. Officers that claim they "feared" for their lives in the presence of a Black man are often projecting internalized implicit biases wherein they view Black men as threatening superhumans, even in nonthreatening situations. The claim that police are afraid may be true, but the reasons for that fear often have nothing to do with the victims being threatening. As police respond to perceived threats of danger within a culture that rewards "bravery" and machismo, law enforcement attracts thrill-seeking behavior that can be detrimental to police and the American people for whom they serve. This hypermasculine subculture, galvanized by fear, serves as a template for the legitimacy of the militarization of American police forces, access to military-grade weapons and vehicles, and a "warrior" mentality (Balko 2014).

Consequently, the media has become inundated with clips, articles, videos, and more that showcase the unnecessary killings of Black men and women by way of excessive use of force and military-influenced tactics. Michael Brown, for example, is but one in a shamefully long list of Black, unarmed men killed at the hands of police (Flatow 2014b). Current police training exacerbates psychological biases toward Black men and encourages use of excessive force (Rosenbaum 2007). Unfortunately, law and policies are structured and enforced to protect and benefit police officers, especially in circumstances in which police are at fault. Police are unlikely to be held accountable in such instances as the law fails to protect the rights and liberties of its citizens while favoring the interests of police and other law enforcement agents.

THE PROTESTS OF SUMMER OF 2020

Protests have broken out more recently in response to the police killing of Breonna Taylor and George Floyd. Police responded to these protests with a militaristic approach, in both gear and use of force, while the media corroborated police efforts by shaping the narrative that protest participants are dangerous and violent rioters (Flatow 2014b). The protests during the summer of 2020 in response to the brutal killings of Floyd and Taylor contrast police presence and use of force in urban neighborhoods with that in suburban neighborhoods. Officers dressed in military-issued riot gear have deployed tear gas in urban neighborhoods where protests have taken place, while they are shown standing alongside White people in more suburban neighborhoods. Today's technological advancements, particularly with respect to smart phones and social media, have allowed the public to record and disseminate accounts of botched raids, police brutality, and unjust killings at the hands of officers. The recorded killing of George Floyd, for example, went viral and rallied people across the nation, sparking protests and inciting demands for both justice and police reform. Consequently, law enforcement has come under fire due to increased public awareness of the rampant abuses of power presently plaguing American policing—leading to increased investigations into the appropriateness of police tactics and force (Balko 2014). However, whether the increased public criticism of police will elicit any substantive change remains unknown.

CHAPTER 8

Black Liberation, the Abolition Movement, and Where We Go from Here

> I continue to be surprised at how little Black lives matter. And I will continue that. Stop giving up on black life. Black people. I love you. I love us. Our lives matter.
>
> —Alicia Garza

On July 13, 2013, after George Zimmerman was acquitted for the murder of Trayvon Martin, the now-founders of the Black Lives Matter movement, Opal Tometi, Patrisse Cullors, and Alicia Garza birthed the Black Lives Matter hashtag that incited a crusade for Black equity and social justice. Black Lives Matter was born out of a national climate of racial disparities in the criminal justice system, the mass incarceration of Black people, the overpolicing of Black people and Black spaces, and the increased militarization of police departments in the United States. Since then, Black Lives Matter chapters have emerged in cities and towns across the United States as well as in countries across the globe in response to local and national state-sanctioned violence at the hands of police officers and extrajudicial vigilante groups.

One of the galvanizing moments for the Black Lives Matter global movement was the Ferguson uprising on August 10, 2014, also referred to as the Ferguson protests or Ferguson riots. On this date, officer Darren Wilson murdered Michael Brown and sparked nationwide turmoil. The unrest in Ferguson grew after a grand jury decided not to indict Darren Wilson on November 24, 2014. In support of Ferguson residents on the ground, Tometi, Cullors, and Garza understood that what was happening in Ferguson was not an anomaly but a reflection of systemic racial violence across the country and around the world. Black liberation leaders left Ferguson to create Black Lives Matter chapters in their own cities and towns and soon after, the Black Lives Matter global network was born. The Black Lives Matter movement has no central "leaders" but is a network of people working toward liberation for all by way of eradicating White supremacy, homophobia, transphobia, patriarchy, and nationalism. Black Lives Matter intentionally centers Black queer and trans women as leaders so as to not replicate patterns of oppression seen in other movement spaces—as mentioned on the Black Lives Matter website: "We affirm the lives of Black queer and trans folks, disabled folks, undocumented folks, folks with records, women, and all Black lives along the gender spectrum. Our network centers those who have been marginalized within Black liberation movements" (Black Lives Matter n.d.).

After the fatal shooting of unarmed Michael Brown in 2014, a postinvestigation report found that the FBI undercounted fatal police shootings by more than half because police reporting is voluntary and many departments fail to do so ("Fatal Force" 2022). In terms of prison demographics, Whites make up 30 percent of the prison population, Latinos 23 percent, and Blacks 33 percent. Black people are, arguably, the population most affected by mass incarceration as they constitute only 12 percent of the U.S. population but more than one-third of the prison population (Kushner 2019).

Almost one in four Black men under the age of thirty-five in Princeton, New Jersey, report being treated unfairly by police after thirty days of being polled. In that same study, Black people report having faced the most unfair treatment while shopping, followed by traffic incidents, and in public entertainment spaces such as theaters or restaurants (Newport 2013). Drakulich (2013) contextualizes perceptions of police by Black and minoritized people through the lens of social control and with consideration to the socioeconomic disadvantages that disproportionately affect their communities. Racial bias on the behalf of police, apparent through practices such as racial profiling, leads to a greater distrust of police by Black people (Weitzer and Tuch 2005). This distrust may lead to more frequent or more severe confrontations between police and citizens. Weitzer and Tuch (2005) contend that White Americans tend to view the police as allies and offer robust support for them. It is also important to acknowledge that half of White people in a 2000 general social-survey report believe Black people to be more inclined to act with criminal or violent intent and condone the police's racialized suspicion toward Black people, referring to it as "rational discrimination." Weitzer and Tuch contend that because most White people view the racialized mistreatment of Black and minoritized people as sensible, when law enforcement is criticized,

White people may perceive this to also be an indirect threat to their group interests. A connection can be made between this notion and the Black Lives Matter (BLM) and the Blue Lives Matter movements, the movements positioned in opposition to one another. For contextual purposes, the BLM movement serves to raise awareness about systemic police brutality and racial injustices persistently plaguing the criminal justice system. The Blue Lives Matter movement, on the other hand, was developed in direct response to the BLM movement and argues that BLM undermines the livelihood of police and elicits a sort of backlash resulting in violence against police and further fuels mistrust of police. The point of contention between these two movements is whether Black people are more likely to experience violence at the hands of police at a greater rate in comparison to any other racial group in the United States (Kramer et al. 2017, 21). The rise of participation in social-justice movements, in response to the brutal killings of Black people at the hands of police, reflects a difference in perception and experience toward police as the racial disparity is increasingly evident and unavoidable in today's age of technology. This is perhaps because African Americans are, and historically have been, racially targeted by the police through the use and implementation of racialized tools, in tactics and in force, to harm and control Black people. As we have demonstrated throughout this book, the United States is, and has been, fundamentally structured to preserve White privilege and to uphold a racial hierarchy in which African Americans are systemically oppressed and marginalized. As we and other scholars have demonstrated, one of such institutions that systemically functions to oppress Black people is the criminal justice system, which has led to several calls to action ranging from police reform to the full abolition of the police.

Defunding vs. Abolition

"Defund the police!" became a popular rallying cry during the summer of 2020 following the police murders of George Floyd and Breonna Taylor, but the movement to defund the police began long before then. In fact, calls to defund the police began as early as 1935 when W. E. B. Du Bois advocated for what he called "abolition-democracy" in his essay "Black Reconstruction" (Du Bois 1936), and scholar and activist Angela Davis has been calling for police abolition since the 1960s. But what does it really mean to defund the police? Defunding the police calls for budgeting significantly less money for police and, instead, investing the funds in other public safety strategies and community resources, such as education, housing, and mental health clinics (Vermeer et al. 2020).

The term abolition is an intentional nod to the movement to abolish slavery

(Kushner 2019). In practice, police abolitionists, too, call for the defunding of police, but, in contrast, call for the gradual disbanding of police units as they presently exist and instituting more humane alternatives to policing in which case police would cease to exist entirely. The notion that police alone are best suited to address social problems, such as local crime, drug abuse, mental health issues, and other social service-based issues, is inherently problematic and for this reason abolitionists call for its imminent disbandment.

Both ideas of defunding the police and abolishing the police are generally quite controversial, though opinion polls and surveys suggest that revisiting and redefining the role of police in society is far less controversial (Vermeer et al. 2020). Vermeer and others (2020) argue that with consideration for this highly polarized era in U.S. history, a common ground might be found in reforms that have a chance of being successful. However, abolitionists address why and how both reform and defunding alone are insufficient.

THE ABOLITION MOVEMENT

As video accounts of police brutality continue to erupt nationwide, criticisms of policing and witness accounts of police brutality are no longer contained within the African American community, but loudly voiced from people from different racial, ethnic, and social classes (Durr 2015). Criticism of law enforcement, especially as it affects the Black community, is not limited to those whom it directly affects but also comes from academics, lawyers, organizers, activists, policy-makers, politicians, and journalists from diverse racial and ethnic backgrounds. Since the murders of Breonna Taylor in March 2020, George Floyd in May 2020, and Rayshard Brooks in June 2020, hundreds of thousands of people have taken to the streets in cities across the United States and countries around the world demanding justice for Black people everywhere.

The summer of 2020 led to a series of "die-ins," protests, marches, riots, teach-ins, as well as the shutting down of highways, major thoroughfares, and public places all in an attempt to demand justice for Black people nationwide in the United States. No longer are organizers and activists simply calling for reform; they are instead demanding the defunding of police departments, reinvestment in community infrastructure, and the eventual end to policing as we know it. Abolitionists call for the ultimate end of policing so as to ensure one oppressive system is not replaced with another one equally or perhaps more oppressive. The movement of prison abolition is, for the most part, led by Black women, Black feminists more specifically, who have historically worked to see their visions of changing the structure of society to benefit all (Kushner 2019).

During the late 1960s and early 1970s, the abolition movement gained traction among scholars, policy-makers, legislators, religious leaders, and others. Three main goals outlined in prison minister Fay Honey Knopp's booklet titled, "Instead of Prisons: A Handbook for Abolitionists" include establishing a moratorium on all new prison buildings, moving away from criminalization, and moving away from the use of incarceration all together (cited in Kushner 2019). The path to achieving these goals consists of generating millions of new jobs, combating employment discrimination, desegregating schools, broadening the social safety net, and building new housing. Unfortunately, by the mid-1960s, the impact of deindustrialization yielded significant negative impacts on urban communities, which was met with harsh forms of criminalization rather than much-needed social programs. By the 1990s, prison complexes and prison populations were exploding nationally, prompting a new call for abolitionists in working to stop states from constructing and building more prisons. In California alone, between 1982 and 2000, twenty-three new prisons were built and increased the prison populations by 500 percent. One of the more successful organizations in this fight is Californians United for a Responsible Budget (CURB), which has prevented over a hundred and forty thousand new jails and prison beds. More recently, CURB, along with the help of several local groups, successfully halted the development and construction of a massive new women's jail in Los Angeles. One clarification worth making is that private prisons are not the "real" or primary problem with mass incarceration: public prisons are of equal concern, and 99 percent of those in jail are in public jails and 92 percent of people in American prisons are held in publicly run, publicly funded facilities. It can be asserted that private prisons, however, more clearly demonstrate to the public the ways in which prisons are part of the larger global capitalist system. Abolitionists critique this assertion in arguing that while state agencies may not profit, they, instead, are tasked with competing for revenue; herein lies the issue. Funding for social welfare shrinks in competition with police, firefighters, and corrections services (Kushner 2019).

Abolitionists call for the significant reduction of police funding by way of suspending use of paid administrative leave for cops under investigation, withholding of pensions, and not rehiring cops that have a history of use of excessive force. They also call for cops to be liable for misconduct settlement, the capping of overtime accrual and overtime pay for military exercises, the withdrawal of participation in police militarization programs, the prioritizing of spending on community resources, and reducing of the size of police forces. In this way, abolitionists challenge the notion that police increase public safety, work toward reducing the scale of policing, and reduce the technology and tools police have at their disposal (Critical Resistance 2014b). In contrast, reformists increase funding to the police by way of body cameras, increase the size and scale of policing, hire more officers, and implement more training that not only fails to lead to positive change for communities but also reinforces the prison-industrial complex (*Critical Resistance* 2014a). The critique reformists face is that they fail to address underlying community issues and further deplete community resources by redirecting and allotting more funding to police departments that are already failing to effectively serve their communities. Simply put, abolitionists argue that many methods of reform reinforce the system rather than reduce incarceration numbers or elicit productive change. Kushner (2019) references the First Step Act, signed into law in 2018, which was to result in the release of seven thousand of the 2.3 million people currently imprisoned in federal prisons, 2.3 million being less than 10 percent of the nation's prison population. Within its first year, more than three thousand people were released and as of July 2022, a total of seven thousand, five hundred inmates have been released (Ortiz 2022). Ruth Wilson Gilmore—director at the Center for Place, Culture, and Politics at the Graduate Center of the City University of New York (CUNY), and author of *Golden Gulag* (2007) and *Change Everything* (2022), and prison abolitionist—contends that the very debate concerning which people ought to be released from prison is both a moral and practical error. To end mass incarceration, ACLU campaign director of Smart Justice, Udi Ofer, argues that the way the system responds to all offenses must be transformed. Ofer, too, recognizes how difficult of a conversation this is politically, but emphasizes moral clarity in the direction the nation must go in working to dismantle the prison system. Many of the proposed efforts of reform consider the prison system as an institution that can be fixed by removing some elements and replacing them with other, similar elements that are often equally as devastating. Abolitionists argue that, rather than try to fix the unfixable, focus ought to be placed on policy work to reduce the carceral system's scope by halting new prison construction, closing prisons, and closing jails by way of grassroots organizing. Ofer argues that incarceration does not work and that Smart Justice aims to defund the prison system and reinvest in communities. The organization's goal is to reduce prison population by 50 percent through local, state, and federal initiatives (Kushner 2019).

The penitentiary movement in the United States throughout the 19th century fed demand for more humanitarian punishment, which is difficult to digest for anyone that is privy to the fact that prisons not only violate human rights and fail to effectively rehabilitate, but their efficacy in deterring crime or increasing public safety is widely undetermined (Kushner 2019). Nonetheless, at the time, prisons were posited as vehicles of reform. Prisons served as a band-aid to social problems. Presently, the United States is the epicenter of incarceration, and attention has been increasingly drawn to the country's state of mass incarceration and the systems for which they are upheld. Mariame Kaba—prison abolitionist, founder and director of Project Nia, and founder of Survived and Punished—urges the United States to critically examine and dismantle the present system of what she refers to as the "criminal punishment system" (Hayes 2019). There is a direct correlation between increased numbers of political prisoners and the imprisonment of poor people of color (Davis and Rodriguez 2000). Despite attempts to posit prisons as rehabilitation-oriented, they more accurately serve to perpetuate poverty and racism. Prisons serve the interests of wealthy Whites who invest in prison stocks and thus depend on the continued imprisonment of Black people to generate revenue. Davis and Rodriguez argue that we must, too, critically examine the political economy of a prison system that benefits from the imprisonment of marginalized people. There are tangible and undeniable political implications to the growing prison-industrial complex. Nixon's war on drugs, for example, was a highly politicized event with grave implications for Black communities, which we will continue to see for decades to come. The repercussions of these politicized maneuvers bleed into a range of socioeconomic issues that impact the upward socioeconomic mobility of Black communities, including residential segregation, health care, education, and so much more. Understanding that crime is not, as conventionally posited, an isolated, individual instance of "deviance" forces us to question the very conditions of criminality for which political rationales deem it appropriate to house an exorbitant number of Black citizens at the behest of capitalist profit. The prison-industrial complex effectively removes large numbers of poor Black people from civil society and criminalizes behavior in certain neighborhoods while ignoring such in more privileged, non-Black neighborhoods.

Consequently, upon release, ex-prisoners suffer social isolation resulting from the criminal labeling, face housing and employment opportunity restrictions, and are exempt from exercising rights such as voting. The prison-industrial complex creates a cyclical pattern of prison re-entry by way of limiting ones' ability to access resources that would otherwise allow for ex-prisoners positively contributing to society; this pattern fuels America's capitalist driven machine—prison. To better contextualize, only 150,000 people were imprisoned at the onset of Nixon's presidency, but by the year 2000, roughly two million people were entrapped in the cycle of the prison system (Davis and Rodriguez 2000). Most of the two million prisoners are Black people, a fact that ought to give one considerable pause (Kushner 2019). This speaks to a culmination of factors, including Nixon's war on drugs and the militarization of police, that ultimately perpetuate and benefit from racial-residential segregation. The call to abolish prisons and police sounds overtly radical, until you do a deeper dive into the mechanisms that prisons and police depend on—the criminalization of Black people. Simply put, it has become abundantly clear that prisons do not accomplish what they proport to accomplish (Kushner 2019), and one would be remiss not to acknowledge the role capitalism plays in the prison-industrial complex.

Capitalism drives many, if not all, of the institutions and systems in the United States, which are further conflated by policy and political power. Racial capitalism remains the driving force behind housing policies and practices that, most recently, have stripped and extracted wealth from Black people in the housing market. For example, subprime-mortgage lending began in Black communities in the late 1990s, and Black folks have suffered disproportionate loss of housing wealth following the collapse of the economy in 2008 and 2009. Moreover, the privatized public education in cities via the school-choice movement continues to privilege White children's education over that of children of color. Removing the capitalist element of the prison-industrial complex would, hypothetically, contribute to its collapse; of course, addressing the underlying "isms," racism and classism for example, is an essential component.

When one calls the police on Black people, the lives of those Black people are quite literally at risk. White folks that call the police against Black people fail to recognize the recklessness of that action. Perhaps this is because White folks do not wholly understand that their experiences with the police are drastically different than those of someone who is non-White. In an interview with Chris Hayes (2019), prison abolitionist Mariame Kaba speaks to this in stating, "by calling the cops, you've . . . like, you've thrown a grenade. You've thrown a grenade and you didn't need to." Taking into consideration what we know about police interactions with Black people and rates of police killings in predominately Black communities, Kaba's statement comes as no shock.

One relevant example is the "Central Park jogger" incident in which a White woman was beaten and raped in New York City in 1989 (Hayes 2019). The consequences of the public wrath that ensued resulted in the unjust, disgraceful imprisonment of five wholly innocent Black children. The process by which these children were interrogated was an infringement on their basic rights of just procedure. The public pressure for law enforcement to prosecute someone for the attack of a White woman resulted in the imprisonment of innocent Black children—the most vulnerable and easily criminalizable and, therefore, easiest of targets. Unfortunately, this incident is not isolated and is grounded in the reality that Black men and boys have historically been criminalized, tortured, and killed in the name of "protecting" White women. All too often, Black people are found innocent for crimes they were wrongly convicted of and served time for despite pleading for their cases to be reopened, a process that is not only lengthy but also expensive.

During the late 1980s through the 1990s, thousands of Black people were imprisoned for both violent and nonviolent crimes, resulting in the largest and most robust incarceration systems the world has come to see. Hayes contends that, yes, we must examine the policies that maintain the prison-industrial system, but we must, first, unpack the root of the problem which begs the question: Why do we punish to the extent and extremity that we do? Who gets punished is not always indicative of how the law is meant to be carried out because the criminal justice system was built upon foundations of racism, classism, and capitalism.

Affluent people residing in wealthier neighborhoods abuse drugs and commit crimes to the same extent as less affluent people, but they are not policed to the degree that Black people are in poorer neighborhoods. Black people who live in poor neighborhoods and use and sell at the same rate or less as wealthy non-White people are jailed far more often and receive far harsher punishments. Herein, we must recognize the ways in which race, class, and racial-residential segregation intersect to inform who receives punishment. Black political organizers and leaders who presented demands to the capital during the crack epidemic were dismissed and overlooked. Their demands were met with more funding allotted to cops, rather than meeting or at very least hearing the demands of Black people. The crime bill of the 1990s had unyielding consequences for Black communities, namely upward of $9 billion allotted for the construction of new prisons—prisons that were filled quickly by members of marginalized communities (Hayes 2019).

Prison abolition is a movement consisting of long-term goals and policies that call for greater government investment in jobs, education, housing, health care, mental health, and other resources necessary for "violence-free" communities. Prison abolition is not simply a means to closing prisons, but rather a means to creating and nurturing vital systems of support for which its absence contributes to higher rates of crime and violence (Kushner 2019). The concept of prison abolition is often met with opposition whereby critics argue it is both unrealistic and radical. Prison abolitionists are flooded with questions related to ensuring safety and whose responsibility it will be to handle threats or emergencies. This resistance is derived from a social consensus that posits policing as the only viable means of ensuring community safety. Abolitionists counter this ideology through advocacy for better, more equitable systems of community support led by folks and organizations that are better equipped to handle community issues and safely de-escalate situations without need for the lethal force we see employed by police departments. Simply put, Williams and others (2019) from the *Star Tribune* argue that we must look beyond police for community safety. The argument here, and most abolition workers will agree, is that a police-first approach is ineffective and fails to address underlying causes of crime. Communities are calling for less police funding and the redirection of funding to alternative community entities and safety measures. Using the Minneapolis Police Department as an example, Williams and others reveal that the department receives $189 million annually in funding; they contextualize the magnitude of this amount by stating that the police budget alone is more than that of the health department, department of civil rights, and community planning and economic development combined. Williams and others share that the department's funds are ill-spent; stings aimed at poor Black men for low-level marijuana sales are carried out, EMS personnel are pressured into drugging community members with ketamine, and hundreds of sexual assault cases are underinvestigated. Not only are police ineffective in keeping communities safe, but the relationship between police-force size and crime levels is statistically insignificant. Decades of research indicate that the biggest contributor to violent crimes is poverty. The traditional police-first approach is ineffective in ensuring public safety; it also inflates underlying causes of crime and contributes to the United States' status as the most incarcerated country in the world.

Abolitionists seek more effective and fiscally responsible means of addressing underlying issues to ensure community safety. Investment in public safety solutions led by experts is one solution aimed at remedying the present climate of unchecked police brutality and ineffective tactics. Kaba implores us to acknowledge that the current political movement encourages an immediate visceral response, which is often not well thought out in terms of future repercussions. This results in criminal-punishment policies that generalize and govern people based on reactionary, extrapolated personal feelings. The term "criminalblackman," coined by Catherine Russel, speaks to the image America has painted of who is criminal and who should be subject to punitive regimes of punishment (Hayes 2019). This leaves all the perpetrators that do not fit the script seemingly invisible and, therefore, undersurveilled.

The recent police killing of Walter Wallace Jr. on Monday, October 26, 2020, supports the notion that police are ill-equipped to de-escalate civilian matters related to mental health. With civilians experiencing mental health crises, people specializing in mental health are far better equipped to handle these cases. According to his mother, Wallace Jr. was experiencing a bipolar episode and was found holding a knife at the time of his death. After unsuccessfully trying to calm Wallace Jr. down, his mother called an ambulance in hopes that paramedics might be better equipped to safely de-escalate the situation. Tragically, the police arrived before the paramedics and acted quickly in firing approximately twelve shots and fatally injuring Wallace Jr. Critics argue that the police could have de-escalated the situation without lethal force, such as employing a taser or simply waiting for the paramedics to arrive before acting (Paybarah and Diaz 2020). This case is one among many that begs the question, What would it look like to fund public services that specialize in mental health and are equipped to support individuals in need of intervention? As is the case with most other resources, mental health services are far more accessible and affordable for more affluent groups of people, whereby rehabilitation and other therapeutic support are more easily attainable. In contrast, poorer communities that do not have the access nor means to seek proper rehabilitation and therapy become entrapped in the criminal justice system—a system ill-equipped to support those struggling with mental health issues. Rather than treating mental health issues as health issues, the United States treats them as criminal issues. The same is true for homelessness and addiction. Herein, proper funding and equitable distribution of vital resources is essential, particularly in neighborhoods misleadingly labeled as "crime-ridden neighborhoods." The term "misleadingly" is important here in recognition of the fact that no neighborhood is inherently crime- ridden; rather, they suffer the consequences of what racial-residential segregation has done to isolated Black communities.

Abolitionists contend that rather than criminalize those who deviate from societal expectations, we must assess the structural issues that complicate or exacerbate criminal actions. Kaba asserts that the voices that are heard by policymakers have racial and class implications, not equitably reflective of all victims but rather the more privileged—it is the more privileged voices that are heard and met with favorable political action (Hayes 2019). These realizations are what have led Kaba to reach her political commitments to transformative justice and restorative justice.

The Transformative-Justice Movement

The theory of transformative organizing is based on a foundation of class consciousness, political leadership, and revolutionary organization comprising seven tenets. These tenets are as follows: (1) transformative justice seeks radical social change through the strategy of building an international unity front to challenge U.S. empire; (2) transformative organizers are conscious agents of change and revolutionary educators; (3) transformative organizing requires the leadership of society's most exploited, oppressed, and strategically placed classes and races; (4) transformative organizing is produced by transformative organizations; (5) transformative organizing becomes truly transformative in the course of battle; (6)

transformative organizing transforms the organizers; (7) transformative organizing requires a transformative political program (Mann 2010). Organizing in the United States is believed to reflect the nation's political climate in which three primary approaches are identified in driving social change. These approaches include (1) right-wing organizing, (2) pragmatic organizing that fights specific reforms in the interest of working people but is limited in scope and characterized by antileft ideology, and (3) left-wing organizing as characterized by militant opposition to racism, war, and abuses of empire—the latter of these approaches is also referred to as transformative organizing. Transformative organizing in the United States began with early slave rebellions in Virginia in opposition to European genocidal conquest and continued with abolitionists and radical Republicans in the 19th century who constitutionally outlawed slavery.

Restorative justice is a concept popularized in the 1970s by Howard Zare but conceived of in Indigenous communities as a peace-making strategy aimed at resolving communal problems. Restorative justice consists of a community of people with a shared set of ideologies and visions of the world who determine the ways in which they will interact with one another when harm is inflicted. This concept centers people that are harmed with respect to the harm being seen, valued, and addressed. The community is called upon to support the person who has been harmed and invites the person that inflicted the harm into conversations that prioritize restoration and accountability. Unlike the present system, restorative justice does not involve, nor rely on, the state because the state and its respective policies have proved to inflict far more lasting harm. The current system operates within the binary of good or bad, rather than acknowledging the gray areas that exist (Hayes 2019). In contrast, restorative justice acknowledges gray areas and offers grace to its community members. Kaba explains that harm brings to light needs and those needs should be met to achieve a state of healing. Hayes argues that restorative justice is far more achievable and implementable than one at first assumes. Despite its alien nature to those unfamiliar with the concept, Kaba contends that we engage in restorative justice in our more intimate relationships quite frequently.

It is reasonable to assert that the fear that comes with notions of dismantling the present policing system stems from the idea that doing so would incite absolute anarchy. Baseless fear aside, one thing is undeniably clear: the system that currently exists is overwhelmingly ineffective and inflicts far more harm than necessary. The criminal justice system fails to discourage deviant behavior, address the underlying social issues of crime, rehabilitate those who have caused harm, and protect all communities. For example, of roughly one thousand rape cases, about two hundred people actually report being raped (Hayes 2019). Of that two hundred, roughly twenty are taken on by a prosecutor and less than five people are convicted. Reallocating money to a restorative-justice model might alter people's views once results are more realistically achievable. At present, the hundreds of billions of dollars allotted to state resources allow for very little funding left for restorative-justice models.

The Justice-Reinvestment Movement

Coined by Susan Tucker and Erica Cadora in 2003, justice reinvestment is posited as a radical intervention into the problem of mass incarceration by way of rearranging public-safety funding. Tucker and Cadora's initial proposal contends that if rates of imprisonment could be reduced, the remaining monetary savings can be reinvested in social services and infrastructure development in high-crime communities (Austin et. al 2016; O'Hear 2016). Justice reinvestment would allow for ensuring public safety in the longer term, as opposed to existing and rigid enforcement-based strategies (O'Hear 2016). Tucker and Cadora stake their claim in favor of the justice-reinvestment model by arguing that the public-safety rationale that the growth of the prison-industrial complex depends on is wholly misleading. They further argue that prison growth has been produced by jailing a growing number of the nation's most disadvantaged communities, with the imprisonment of said community members eroding human and social capital within those areas. The increased financial costs of the growing prison system have reduced the government's ability to invest in the much-needed human and social-capital infrastructures for the communities most impacted, and significant reductions in prison populations is, in fact, achievable without jeopardizing public safety. Two central themes can be derived from this argument. First, penalties and punishment within the United States have grown entirely out of proportion to what is fair or just. Second, the growing prison system disproportionately negatively impacts marginalized communities and, consequently, produces intergenerational patterns of prison cycling that further erode socioeconomic resources (Austin et. al 2016).

Somewhat surprisingly, the justice-reinvestment model has become broadly accepted as an attractive strategy for addressing mass incarceration, creating large reductions in imprisonment costs, and redirecting public funding toward communities that have been impacted by crime and incarceration. Justice reinvestment is supported and directed by the Council of State Governments, Pew Charitable Trust, the Vera Institute of Justice, and, more recently, the U.S. Department of Justice. The Bureau of Justice Assistance reports that, as of 2016, twenty-seven states are officially involved in the justice-reinvestment movement in some capacity (Austin et. al 2016).

CONSIDER: THE PRESENT SYSTEM HURTS COPS, TOO

In the United States, a single entity has been assigned the task of addressing a diverse range of social problems that otherwise require responses from practitioners with very specialized training and experience. It is simply unrealistic and ineffective to task a single institution with addressing such a vast range of social inequities that they are unable to effectively remedy. In what ways, we must then ask, is the criminal justice system as it presently operates failing its own officers as well? Most of the issues police face are undoubtedly layered and derived from insufficient community resources. Asking them to serve in place of social workers, emergency mental health professionals, or medical professionals without proper training increases the risk of officers being emotionally and mentally overwhelmed. In doing so, we are simply setting officers up for failure. One must consider how the present system inflicts harm on officers and in turn the community that they are assigned to serve. The Unites States' system of law enforcement has created a toxic cycle of individuals ill-equipped to address many of the social issues they come into contact with. Vermeer and others suggest that officers can suffer from the vicarious trauma of repeatedly responding to the consequences of homelessness, drug abuse, and mental health crises. Further complicating this discussion is the police culture surrounding mental health in which seeking mental health care is widely frowned upon and, unsurprisingly, results in volatile, improperly trained individuals policing communities that are perpetually overpoliced and segregated.

Critical Race Theory, Antiracist Curricula, and Public Education

Of course, policing as an institution does not stand alone as the sole enforcer of White supremacy and the U.S. racial-caste system, but works in tandem with housing, education, and a broad range of other institutions. Not only have we seen policy legislation and social movements aimed at defunding and abolishing the U.S. system of policing, but also movement to overhaul our existing education system as well. A culmination of recent events, protests, and movements in response to continued police brutality has given rise to a push for more inclusive, antiracist pedagogy in America's public schools. Advocates of antiracist educational practices address both the academic and socio-emotional implications of racism within the school setting and strive to center social justice. There is a resounding call for the development and inclusion of antiracist curricula that effectively informs students of America's racist history. As Hayter (cited in Simon 2021) notes, we must veer away from a romanticized version of America's past in which we erase the uglier truths of our racist foundation. Doing so requires that we rethink and reshape contemporary curricula to unveil the racial underpinnings of America's history. This, however, cannot be accomplished without antiracism being a core facet of the process.

While the magnet school system was designed to desegregate schools, it fails to address the very root of how school segregation and unequal resource distribution has been maintained over time. Magnet schools largely exist as a means to correct segregation in public schools, despite the ensuing White flight that often occurs in White or integrated districts that have magnet schools (Rossell 2003). That most American students attending magnet and charter schools do not understand what differentiates their schools from others, or why they must be bused to schools outside their districts to experience racial diversity, highlights the extent to which systemic racism is built into educational institutions and speaks to the lengths to which policy-makers will go to conceal the depths of America's racist history. Even in educational settings born out of an inherent need to correct systemic segregation, we fail to educate our students as to *why* these vehicles of desegregation exist. Framing it this way ought to elicit a moment of "Aha!" But entire groups of people across this nation are in active opposition of the incorporation of antiracist curricula in American schools as it threatens the very core of White American superiority, entitlement, and the myth of meritocracy they continue to buy into.

Not only are some White Americans resisting the incorporation of inclusive and antiracist pedagogy in schools, but they specifically name Critical Race Theory (CRT) as the main culprit in advancing this mission, despite having very little understanding of what CRT is and its relationship to, or lack thereof, the pedagogy that educators wish to implement. This pushback comes as no surprise when considering that the vast majority of American citizens have been sold an idealized tale of America's heritage, rather than factual, reasoned accounts of the nation's history. As such, restructuring American curricula to effectively incorporate and address the nation's history of racism comes across as a shock to the system and is often misperceived as an abrasive, politicized move to ostracize Whites. This is in part because the general population does not understand what CRT is: originating in the 1970s, CRT argues that racism is the vehicle through which we have crafted and enforced American policy, laws, and culture (Coaston 2021). Jane Coaston contextualizes its misconception in arguing, "If you listen to the news you might think that critical race theory is a school curriculum, or a workplace diversity training, or a form of discrimination, or Marxist propaganda. It's none of the above." As is the case with movements to alternative policing, such as defunding, the push for antiracist curricula has become overwhelmingly politicized. As Democrats and Republicans are pitted against one another, we find ourselves further distracted from the true nature of CRT and its inherent need within the educational sphere of American culture. Former president Donald Trump, while unsuccessful, tried to eradicate federal training that included CRT and galvanized his followers to follow suit, leading to a lumping of all antiracist pedagogy under the CRT umbrella. Coaston argues that the true nature of the issue at hand has nothing to do with CRT itself, but rather the intersection of extensions of power, capital, and business. While the urgency of CRT is often associated with the BLM protests of 2020, Zach Goldberg (2020, in Coaston 2021) discovered that CRT language had been slowly but surely making its way into the collective consciousness of American society well before Trump's time in office and the murder of George Floyd. Coaston argues that CRT has, in fact, already crept into school curricula and instruction across the nation as schools have made a more intentional effort to acknowledge antiracist movements. Despite this, CRT and antiracist work within the school setting has become increasingly weaponized as a political tool in service to the right-wing agenda.

A Cautionary Tale: Organized White Supremacy, Trump, and the Growth of the Alt-Right

As we have shown throughout this book, while race is certainly a social construct, race has a tangible impact on the lives of people living in the United States, especially as it pertains to how one is treated by our systems of law enforcement, housing, and public education. Moreover, the social construction of race is not something that "happened" but something that continues to evolve as some work to double down on "Whiteness"—carving an even more exclusionary identity regarding who "belongs" and who does not. Others work to undo the harm that Whiteness has inflicted upon the whole of society. We hope that what you have gained from this book is a new perspective—to see not only how these forces have worked historically but also, through a contextualization of historical events, how they continue to operate and mutate within our current systems. Omi and Winant (1994) talk of racial projects as "both a reflection of and response to the broader patterning of race in the overall social system," and say that "every racial project attempts to reproduce, extend, subvert, or directly challenge that system." This extends both to moments of subverting the racial status quo and upholding it. As we see the growth of abolition, progressive racial politics, and the call to divest in policing and reinvest in communities, we also see a rise in alt-right politics, the stripping of civil liberties, and a call to uphold explicitly White supremacist values, policies, and practices. The White supremacist backlash that emerged during the Obama years, crystallized during the Trump presidency, is now building as the alt-right searches for ways to double down on the Trumpian racial project. This backlash is not a mere reaction to the United States' first Black president, nor a mere product of his openly racist successor; rather, it is the product of a much longer history that includes slavery and subsequent ideas about race, what it means to be White, and how to uphold the growing White supremacist system that has informed the United States since its inception.

We must simultaneously hold out hope for a better future while being cautious of the powers that have always worked to oppress, marginalize, and harm. The logic of White supremacy and the institutionalization of racial hierarchy continues to pervade each system, creating mutually reinforcing and compounding conditions of surveillance and criminalization at the expense of people of color.

WORKS CITED

Aalbers, M. B. 2006. "'When the Banks Withdraw, Slum Landlords Take Over': The Structuration of Neighborhood Decline through Redlining, Drug Dealing, Speculation and Immigrant Exploitation." *Urban Studies* 43 (7): 1061–86.

Adelman, R. 2004. "Neighborhood Opportunities, Race, and Class: The Black Middle Class and Residential Segregation." *City & Community* 3:43–63.

———. 2005. "The Role of Race, Class, and Residential Preferences in the Neighborhood Racial Composition of Middle-Class Blacks and Whites." *Social Science Quarterly* 86:209–28.

ACLU of New York. Accessed July 17, 2022. www.nyclu.org/en/stop-and-frisk-data.

Alba, R., and J. Logan. 1991. "Variations on Two Themes: Racial and Ethnic Patterns in the Attainment of Suburban Residence." *Demography* 28:431–53.

Alba, R. J. Logan, B. Stults, G. Marzan, and W. Zhang. 1999. "Immigrant Groups in the Suburbs: A Reexamination of Suburbanization and Spatial Assimilation." *American Sociological Review* 64:446–60.

Alba, R., and V. Nee. 2003. *Remaking the American Mainstream: Assimilation and Contemporary Immigration*. Cambridge, Mass.: Harvard University Press.

Alexander, M. 2010. *The New Jim Crow: Mass Incarceration in the Age of Colorblindness*. New York: New Press.

Allen, T. 1994. *The Invention of the White Race*. Vol. 1. London: Verso.

Almond, M. R. 2012. "The Black Charter School Effect: Black Students in American Charter Schools." *Journal of Negro Education* 81 (4): 354–65.

Allport, G. W., and L. Postman. 1947. *The Psychology of Rumor*. New York: Henry Holt.

Anderson, C. 2021. *The Second: Race and Guns in a Fatally Unequal America*. London: Bloomsbury.

Anderson, E. 2011. *The Cosmopolitan Canopy: Race and Civility in Everyday Life*. New York: Norton.

Anderson, E. 2012. "The Iconic Ghetto." *Annals of the American Academy of Political and Social Science* 642 (1): 8–24.

———. 1999. *Code of the Street: Decency, Violence, and the Moral Life of the Inner City*. New York: Norton.

———. 2016. "Charter School Reform: Doublethink and the Assault on the Vulnerable." *Journal of Thought* 50 (3–4): 33–48.

Archbald, D. A. 2004. "School Choice, Magnet Schools, and the Liberation Model: An Empirical Study." *Sociology of Education* 77 (4): 283–310.

Asante Jr., M. 2008. "What's Really Hood? A Conversation with the Ghetto." In *It's Bigger than Hip Hop: The Rise of the Post-Hip-Hop Generation*, 33–44. New York: St. Martin's.

Austin, J., T. Clear, and G. Coventry. 2016. "Reinvigorating Justice Reinvestment." *Federal Sentencing Reporter* 29 (1): 6–14.

Baird, T. 2015. "Stop the Killing: Fatal Police Shootings in Canada." *Independent*. April 14, 2015. https://theindependent.ca/commentary/a-measured-opinion/stop-the-killing-fatal-police-shootings-in-canada/.

Balko, R. 2014. *Rise of the Warrior Cop: The Militarization of America's Police Forces*. New York: Public Affairs.

Barlow, D. E., and M. H. Barlow. 1999. "A Political Economy of Community Policing." *Policing: An International Journal of Police Strategies and Management* 22:646–74.

Bass, S. 2001. "Policing Space, Policing Race: Social Control Imperatives and Police Discretionary Decisions." *Social Justice* 28 (1): 156–77.

Baum, D. 1996. *Smoke and Mirrors: The War on Drugs and the Politics of Failure*. Boston: Little, Brown.

———. 2016. "Legalize It All: How to Win the War on Drugs." *Harper's Magazine*. April 2016. https://harpers.org/archive/2016/04/legalize-it-all/.

Beger, R. R. 2002. "Expansion of Police Power in Public Schools and the Vanishing Rights of Students." *Social Justice* 29:119–30.

Bekiempis, V. 2014. "How Much Does the NYPD Spend on Misdemeanor Arrests?" *Newsweek*. December 15, 2014. www.newsweek.com/embargoeddec-156-pm-policing-costs-291948.

Bellesiles, M. A. 2002. "Exploring American Gun Culture." *William and Mary Quarterly* 59 (1): 241–68.

Berry, H. 2016. "Militia Group Seizes Malheur National Wildlife Refuge Headquarters." *Boise Weekly*. January 3, 2016. www.idahopress.com/boiseweekly/news/citydesk/militia-group-seizes-malheur-national-wildlife-refuge-headquarters/article_fea4f354-c6fd-54c0-9e72-6838dc103058.html.

Blackmon, D. A. 2009. *Slavery by Another Name: The Re-Enslavement of Black Americans from the Civil War to World War II*. New York: Anchor.

Black Lives Matter. "About." Black Lives Matter. Accessed July 24, 2022. https://blacklivesmatter.com/about/.

Blackwell, B. 2014. "Daughter of Mentally Ill Cleveland Woman Who Died in Custody Hopes for Change." cleveland.com. www.cleveland.com/metro/2014/11/daughter_of_mentally_ill_cleve.html.

Blanchett, W. 2006. "Disproportionate Representation of African American Students in Special Education: Acknowledging the Role of White Privilege and Racism." *Educational Researcher* 35 (6): 24–28.

Blanchett, W. J., and M. W. Shealey. 2005. "The Forgotten Ones: African American Students

with Disabilities in the Wake of *Brown*." In *Brown v. Board of Education: Its Impact on Public Education 1954–2004*, edited by Dara N. Byrne, 213–26. New York: Word for Word.
Blanchett, W. J., V. Mumford, and F. Beachum. 2005. "Urban School Failure and Disproportionality in a Post-Brown era. *Remedial and Special Education* 26:70–81.
Bobo, L., and C. Zubrinsky. 1996. "Attitudes on Residential Integration: Perceived Status Differences, Mere In-Group Preference, or Racial Prejudice?" *Social Forces* 74:883–909.
Bonilla-Silva, E. 2014. *Racism without Racists: Color-Blind Racsim and the Persistence of Racial Inequality in America*. Lanham, Md.: Rowman & Littlefield.
Boyer J. B., and H. P. Baptiste Jr. 1996. *Transforming the Curriculum for Multicultural Understanding: A Practitioner's Handbook*. San Francisco: Caddo Gap Press.
Brantlinger, E. 2003. *Dividing Classes: How the Middle Class Negotiates and Rationalizes School Advantage*. New York: Routledge.
Brooks, K., V. Schiraldi, and J. Ziedenberg. 1999. *School House Hype: Two Years Later*. San Francisco: Center on Juvenile and Criminal Justice.
Brooks-Gunn, J., G. Duncan, P. Klebanov, and N. Sealand. 1993. "Do Neighborhoods Influence Child and Adolescent Development?" *American Journal of Sociology* 99 (2): 353–95.
Brown, J. K., and M. E. Klas. 2014. "Inmate Reports Threats by Guard, Turns Up Dead." *Miami Herald*. www.miamiherald.com/news/state/florida/article2564576.html.
Browning, J. B. 1930. "The North Carolina Black Code. *Journal of Negro History*, 15 (4): 461–73.
Bulwa, D. 2010. "NAACP Focuses on Officer Involved Shootings." *SFGATE*. December 17, 2010. www.sfgate.com/bayarea/article/NAACP-focuses-on-officer-involved-shootings-2453109.php.
Burris, C. C., and K. G. Welner. 2005. "Closing the Achievement Gap by Detracking." *Phi Delta Kappan International* 86 (8): 594-98.
Capers, B. 2009. "Policing, Place, and Race." *Harvard Civil Rights–Civil Liberties Law Review* 44:43–78. https://brooklynworks.brooklaw.edu/cgi/viewcontent.cgi?referer=https://www.google.com/&httpsredir=1&article=1121&context=faculty.
Chambliss, W. J. 1994. "Policing the Ghetto Underclass: The Politics of Law and Law Enforcement." *Social Problems* 41 (2): 177–94.
Chapman, T. K. 2007. "Interrogating Classroom Relationships and Events: Using Portraiture and Critical Race Theory in Education Research." *Educational Researcher* 36(3).
Charles, C. Z. 2000. "Neighborhood Racial-Composition Preferences: Evidence from a Multiethnic Metropolis." *Social Problems* 47:379–407.
———. 2003. "The Dynamics of Racial Residential Segregation." *Annual Review of Sociology* 29 (1): 167–207.
Chen, A. K. 2015. "Qualified Immunity Limiting Access to Justice and Impeding Development of Law." *Human Rights* 41 (1): 8–10.
Civil Rights Data Collection. 2011–12. "2011–12 Civil Rights Data Collection Questions and Answers." U.S. Department of Education. Last modified January 10, 2020. https://www2.ed.gov/about/offices/list/ocr/docs/crdc-2011-12-factsheet.html.
Civil Rights Project, The. 2001. *Discrimination in Special Education*. Cambridge, Mass.: The Civil Rights Project, Harvard University.
Clark, W. 1986. "Residential Segregation in American Cities: A Review and Interpretation." *Population Research and Policy Review* 5:95–127.

Clark, M. A., P. M. Gleason, C. C. Tuttle, and M. K. Silverberg. 2015. "Do Charter Schools Improve Student Achievement?" *Educational Evaluation and Policy Analysis* 37 (4): 419–36.

Coaston, J. 2021. "Does Teaching America It's Racist Make It Less Racist?" *New York Times. The Argument* podcast, 36:04. May 19, 2021. www.nytimes.com/2021/05/19/opinion/race-theory-us-racism.html.

Collins, W. J., and M. H. Wanamaker. 2014. "Selection and Economic Gains in the Great Migration of African Americans: New Evidence from Linked Census Data." *American Economics Journal: Applied Economics* 6 (1): 220–52.

Correll, J., B. Park, C. M. Judd, and B. Wittenrbink. 2002. "The Police Officer's Dilemma: Using Ethnicity to Disambiguate Potentially Threatening Individuals." *Journal of Personality and Social Psychology* 83 (6): 1314–29.

Coviello, D., and N. Persico. 2015. "An Economic Analysis of Black-White Disparities in the New York Police Department's Stop-and-Frisk Program." *Journal of Legal Studies* 44 (2): 315–60.

Critical Resistance. 2014a. *Critical Resistance 2014 Annual Report*. Posted March 27, 2015. https://criticalresistance.org/annual-reports/critical-resistance-in-2014-check-our-annual-report/.

Critical Resistance. 2014b. "Reformist Reforms vs. Abolitionist Steps in Policing." https://criticalresistance.org/wp-content/uploads/2021/08/CR_abolitioniststeps_antiexpansion_2021_eng.pdf.

Cross, B. 2003. "Learning or Unlearning Racism: Transferring Teacher Education Curriculum to Classroom Practices." *Theory into Practice* 42 (3): 203–309.

Crowder, K. 2000. "The Racial Context of White Mobility: An Individual-Level Assessment of the White Flight Hypothesis." *Social Science Research* 29:223–57.

D'Arcy, J. 2012. "Salecia Johnson, 6, Handcuffed after Tantrum: What's Wrong with This Picture?" *Washington Post*. April 18, 2012. www.washingtonpost.com/blogs/on-parenting/post/salecia-johnson-6-handcuffed-after-tantrum-whats-wrong-with-this-picture/2012/04/18/gIQAiUitQT_blog.html.

Darling-Hammond, L. 2004. "Inequality and the Right to Learn: Access to Qualified Teachers in California's Public Schools." *Teachers College Record* 106:1936–66.

Davis, A. J., ed. 2017. *Policing the Black Man: Arrest Prosecution, and Imprisonment*. New York: Pantheon.

Davis, A. Y. 1998. "Race and Criminalization: Black Americans and the Punishment Industry." In *The Angela Y. Davis Reader*, edited by J. Jones, 61–73. Malden, Mass.: Blackwell.

Davis, A. Y., and D. Rodriguez. 2000. "The Challenge of Prison Abolition: A Conversation." *Social Justice* 27 (3): 212–18.

Denton, N., and D. Massey. 1988. "Residential Segregation of Blacks, Hispanics, and Asians by Socioeconomic Status and Generation." *Social Science Quarterly* 69:797–818.

Devine, P. G. 1989. "Stereotypes and Prejudice: Their Automatic and Controlled Components." *Journal of Personality and Social Psychology* 56 (1): 5–18.

Devoe, J. F., K. Peter, M. Noonan, T. D. Snyder, and K. Baum. 2005. *Indicators of School Crime and Safety 2005*. Washington, D.C.: U.S. Department of Education.

Dinkes, R., E. F. Cataldi, and W. Lin-Kelly. 2007. *Indicators of School Crime and Safety: 2007*. Washington, D.C.: U.S. Department of Education.

Dinkes, R., J. Kemp, and K. Baum. 2009. *Indicators of School Crime and Safety: 2008*. Washington, D.C.: National Center for Education Statistics.

Dixon, J. 2006. "The Ties That Bind and Those That Don't: Toward Reconciling Group Threat and Contact Theories of Prejudice." *Social Forces* 84 (4): 2179–204.

Drakulich, K. M., and R. D. Crutchfield. 2013. "The Role of Perceptions of the Police in Informal Social Control: Implications for the Racial Stratification of Crime and Control." *Social Problems* 60 (3):383–407.

Du Bois, W. E. B. 1936. "Black Reconstruction: An Essay Toward the History of the Part Which Black Folk Played in the Attempt to Reconstruct Democracy in America, 1860–1880." *Journal of American History* 23 (2): 278–80.

Dukes, K., and S. E. Gaither. 2017. "Black Racial Stereotypes and Victim Blaming: Implications for Media Coverage and Criminal Proceedings in Cases of Police Violence against Racial and Ethnic Minorities." *Journal of Social Issues* 73 (4):789–807.

Durr, M. 2015. "What Is the Difference between Slave Patrols and Modern Day Policing? Institutional Violence in a Community of Color." *Critical Sociology* 41 (6):1–7.

Dyson, M. E. 2017. *Tears We Cannot Stop: A Sermon to White America*. New York: St. Martin's.

Eberhardt, J. L., P. A. Goff, V. J. Purdie, and P. G. Davies. 2004. "Seeing Black: Race, Crime, and Visual Processing." *Journal of Personality and Social Psychology* 87 (6):876–93.

Ellen, I. G. 2000. *Sharing America's Neighborhoods: The Prospects for Stable Racial Integration*. Cambridge, Mass.: Harvard University Press.

Embrick, D. 2015. "Two Nations, Revisited: The Lynching of Black and Brown Bodies, Police Brutality, and Racial Control in 'Post-Racial' Amerikka." *Critical Sociology* 41 (6):835–43.

Emerson, M. O., Yancey, G., and Chai, K. (2001). "Does Race Matter in Residential Segregation? Exploring the Preferences of White Americans." *American Sociological Review* 66 (6): 922–35.

Entman, R. M., and K. A. Gross. 2008. "Race to Judgement: Stereotyping Media and Criminal Defendants." *Law and Contemporary Problems* 71 (4): 93–133.

Fagan, J., V. West, and J. Hollan. 2003. "Reciprocal Effects of Crime and Incarceration in New York City Neighborhoods." *Fordham Urban Law Journal* 30:1551–99.

Farley, R., H. Schuman, S. Bianchi, D. Colasanto, and S. Hatchett. 1978 "Chocolate City, Vanilla Suburbs: Will the Trend Toward Racially Separate Communities Continue?" *Social Science Research* 7:319–44.

Farley, R., and W. Frey. 1994. "Changes in the Segregation of Whites from Blacks during the 1980s: Small Steps Toward a More Integrated Society." *American Sociological Review* 59 (1): 23–45.

Farley, R., C. Steeh, M. Krysan, T. Jackson, and K. Reeves. 1994. "Stereotypes and Segregation: Neighborhoods in the Detroit Area." *American Journal of Sociology* 100:750–80.

Farley, R., E. Fielding, and M. Krysan. 1997. "The Residential Preferences of Blacks and Whites: A Four-Metropolis Analysis." *Housing Policy Debate* 8:763–800.

"Fatal Force: 1,056 People Have Been Shot and Killed by the Police the Past Year." *Washington Post*. August 18, 2022. https://www.washingtonpost.com/graphics/investigations/police-shootings-database/.

Feagin, J. R. 2006. *Systemic Racism: A Theory of Oppression*. New York: Routledge.

———. 2010. *The White Racial Frame: Centuries of Racial Framing and Counter-Framing*. 2nd ed. New York: Routledge.

Ferguson, A. A. 2001. *Bad Boys: Public Schools in the Making of Black Masculinity*. Ann Arbor: University of Michigan Press.

Fischer, M. J. 2003. "The Relative Importance of Income and Race in Determining Residential Outcomes in US Urban Areas, 1970–2000." *Urban Affairs Review* 38(5): 669–96.

Fitzgerald, K. 2017. *Recognizing Race and Ethnicity: Power, Privilege, and Inequality*. 2nd ed. New York: Routledge.

Flatow, N. 2013. "One in Four Young Black Men Recall Recent Unfair Treatment, Gallup Finds." *ThinkProgress*. July 18, 2013. https://archive.thinkprogress.org/one-in-four-young-black-men-recall-recent-unfair-police-treatment-gallup-finds-20f5ea7b2a08/

———. 2014a. "Report: Black Male Teens Are 21 Times More Likely to be Killed by Cops Than White Ones." *ThinkProgress*. October 10, 2014. https://archive.thinkprogress.org/report-black-male-teens-are-21-times-more-likely-to-be-killed-by-cops-than-white-ones-72fb08a1dbda/.

———. 2014b. "Michael Brown, Police Violence, and Why It's So Hard for Victims to See Justice." *ThinkProgress*. August 12, 2014. https://archive.thinkprogress.org/michael-brown-police-violence-and-why-its-so-hard-for-victims-to-see-justice-23abc0d9a67c/

Fountain, B. 2018. "Slavery and the Origins of the American Police State." GEN (*Medium*). September 17, 2018. https://gen.medium.com/slavery-and-the-origins-of-the-american-police-state-ec318f5ff05b.

Fossett, M. 2006. "Ethnic Preferences, Social Distance Dynamics, and Residential Segregation: Theoretical Explorations Using Simulation Analysis." *Journal of Mathematical Sociology* 30:185–273.

Frankenberg E., and C. Lee. 2003. "Charter Schools and Race: A Lost Opportunity for Integrated Education." *Education Policy Analysis Archives* 11.

Gay, G. 1995. "Mirror Images on Community Issues." In *Multicultural Education, Critical Pedagogy, and the Politics of Difference*, edited by C. Sleeter and P. McLaren, 155–190. Albany: State University of New York Press.

Gilmore, R. W. 2007. *Golden Gulag: Prisons, Surplus, Crisis, and Opposition in Globalizing California*. Chicago: Haymarket.

———. 2022. *Change Everything: Racial Capitalism and the Case for Abolition*. Berkeley: University of California Press.

Giroux, H. A. 2003. "Racial Injustice and Disposable Youth in the Age of Zero Tolerance." *International Journal of Qualitative Studies in Education* 16:553–65.

Glaeser, E. L., J. L. Vigdor. 2001. *Racial Segregation in the 2000 Census: Promising News*. Brookings Institution, Washington, D.C.

———. 2012. "The End of the Segregated Century: Racial Separation in America's Neighborhoods, 1890–2010." *Manhattan Institute for Policy Research* 66. www.manhattan-institute.org/html/end-segregated-century-racial-separation-americas-neighborhoods-1890-2010-5848.html.

Goel, S., J. M. Rao, and R. Shroff. 2016. "Precinct of Prejudice? Understanding Racial Disparities in New York City's Stop-and-Frisk Policy." *Annals of Applied Statistics* 10 (1):365–94.

Goff, P. A., J. L. Eberhardt, M. J. Williams, and M. C. Jackson. 2008. "Not Yyet Human: Implicit Knowledge, Historical Dehumanization, and Contemporary Consequences." *Journal of Personality and Social Psychology* 94 (2): 292–306.

Goldberg, J. A. 2015. "Theorizing and Resisting the Violence of Stop and Frisk-Style Profiling." *CLA Journal* 58(3–4):256–76.

Goldring, E., and C. Smrekar. 2002. "Magnet Schools: Reform and Race in Urban Education." *Clearing House* 76 (1): 13–15.

GHRSCO and CSDE (Greater Hartford Regional School Choice Office and Connecticut State Department of Education). "Quick Reference Guide to School Choice in the Greater Hartford Region: School Year 2022–23; Pre-K to Grade 12." portal.ct.gov. Accessed 24 July 2022. https://portal.ct.gov/-/media/SDE/School-Choice/RSCO/RSCOQuickGuide.pdf.

Hadden, S. E. 2003. *Slave Patrols: Law and Violence in Virginia and the Carolinas*. Cambridge, Mass.: Harvard University Press.

Hayes, C. 2019. "Thinking About How to Abolish Prisons with Mariame Kaba: Podcast & Transcript." NBC News, THINK, *Why Is This Happening?* (podcast). April 10, 2019. www.nbcnews.com/think/opinion/thinking-about-how-abolish-prisons-mariame-kaba-podcast-transcript-ncna992721.

Harcourt, B. E. 2009. *Illusion of Order: The False Promise of Broken Windows Policing*. Cambridge, Mass.: Harvard University Press.

Harris, D. 2001. "Why Are Whites and Blacks Averse to White Neighbors?" *Social Science Research* 30:100–116.

Harry, B. and J. K. Klingner. 2006. *Why Are So Many Minority Students in Special Education? Understanding Race and Disability in Schools*. New York: Teachers College.

Hattery, A. J. and E. Smith. 2018. *Policing Black Bodies: How Black Lives Are Surveilled and How to Work for Change*. Lanham, Md.: Rowman & Littlefield.

Heitzeg, N. A. 2014. "Chapter One: Criminalizing Education: Zero Tolerance Policies, Police in the Hallways, and the School to Prison Pipeline." *Counterpoints* 453:11–36.

Hirschfield, P. J. 2008. "Preparing for Prison? The Criminalization of School Discipline in the USA." *Theoretical Criminology* 12:79–101.

———. 2015. "Lethal Policing: Making Sense of American Exceptionalism." *Sociological Forum* 30 (4): 1109–17.

House, K. 2016. "As Militant Occupation Continues in Oregon, Sheriff Says 'Go Home.'" *OregonLive.com*. January 4, 2016. www.oregonlive.com/pacific-northwest-news/2016/01/as_militant_occupation_continu.html.

Iceland, J., and R. Wilkes. 2006. "Does Socioeconomic Status Matter? Race, Class, and Residential Segregation." *Social Problems* 52 (2): 248–73.

Ingersoll, R. 2004. *Why Do High-Poverty Schools Have Difficulty Staffing Their Classrooms with Qualified Teachers?* Washington, D.C.: Center for American Progress.

Ingersoll, R., L. Merrill, and H. May. 2012. "Retaining Teachers: How Preparation Matters." *Educational Leadership* 69(8): 30–34.

Jackson, T. L. 2009. "Slave Patrols in Edward P. Jones' 'The Known World.'" *College Language Association Journal* 53(2): 162–77.

Jacobson, M. F. 1998. *Whiteness of a Different Color: European Immigrants and the Alchemy of Race*. Cambridge, Mass.: Harvard University Press.

Jargowsky, P. 1994. "Ghetto Poverty among Blacks in the 1980s." *Journal of Policy Analysis and Management* 13(2): 288–310.

———. 1996. "Take the Money and Run: Economic Segregation in U.S. Metropolitan Areas." *American Sociological Review* 61 (6): 984–98.

Johnson, W. 2002. "Slaveholders on Guard." *William and Mary Quarterly* 59 (3): 799–802.

Johnson, C., and S. Gideon. 2015. "Interview on Tanisha Anderson," interview by authors.

From "Say Her Name: Resisting Police Brutality Against Black Women." (https://static1.squarespace.com/static/53f20d90e4b0b80451158d8c/t/5edc95fba357687217b08fb8/1591514635487/SHNReportJuly2015.pdf)

Jones, N. 2009. *Between Good and Ghetto: African American Girls and Inner-City Violence*. Rutgers University Press.

Kang, J. 2005. "Trojan Horses of Race." *Harvard Law Review* 118 (5): 1489–593.

Kelling, G., and J. Wilson. 1982. "Broken Windows: The Police and Neighborhood Safety." *Atlantic*. March 1982. www.theatlantic.com/magazine/archive/1982/03/broken-windows/304465/.

Kendi, I. X. 2019. *How to Be an Anti-Racist*. New York: One World.

Kirshner, B., M. Gaertner, and K. Pozzoboni. 2010. "Tracing Transitions: The Effect of High School Closure on Displaced Students." *Educational Evaluation and Policy Analysis* 32 (3): 407–29.

Kozol, J. 2004. "Beyond Black, White, and Brown." *Nation* 278 (17):17–24.

Kramer, R., B. Remster, C. Z. Charles. 2017. "Black Lives and Police Tactics Matter." *Contexts* 16 (3): 20–25.

Kraska, P. B. 2007. "Militarization and Policing—Its Relevance to 21st Century Police." *Policing: A Journal of Policy and Practice* 1 (4):501–13.

Kraska, P. B., ed. 2001. *Militarizing the American Criminal Justice System: The Changing Roles of the Armed Forces and the Police*. Boston: Northeastern University Press.

Krysan, M. 1998. "Privacy and Expression of White Racial Attitudes: A Comparison across Three Contexts." *Public Opinion Quarterly* 62:506–44.

———. 2002a. "Community Undesirability in Black and White: Examining Racial Residential Preferences through Community Perceptions." *Social Problems* 49: 521–43.

———. 2002b. "Whites Who Said They'd Flee: Who Are They and Why Would They Leave?" *Demography* 39:675–96.

Krysan, M., and M. Bader. 2007. "Perceiving the Metropolis: Seeing the City through a Prism of Race." *Social Forces* 86 (2): 699–733.

Krysan, M., and K. Crowder. 2017. *Cycle of Segregation: Social Processes and Residential Stratification*. Russell Sage Foundation.

Krysan, M., R. Farley, M.P. Cooper, and T.A. Forman. 2009. "Does Race Matter in Neighborhood Preferences? Results from a Video Experiment." *American Journal of Sociology* 115 (2): 527–59.

Kushner, R. 2019. "Is Prison Necessary? Ruth Wilson Gilmore Might Change Your Mind." *New York Times Magazine*. April 17, 2019. www.nytimes.com/2019/04/17/magazine/prison-abolition-ruth-wilson-gilmore.html.

Lane, K. A., J. Kang, and M. R. Banaji. 2007. "Implicit Social Cognition and Law." *Annual Review of Law and Social Science* 3 (1): 427–51.

Langton, L., and M. R. Durose. 2013. *Police Behavior during Traffic and Street Stops, 2011*. Washington, D.C.: U.S. Department of Justice, Office of Justice Programs, Bureau of Justice Statistics.

Lartey, J. 2015. "By the Numbers: U.S. Police Kill More in Days Than Other Countries Do in a Year." *Guardian* (U.S. edition). June 9, 2015. www.theguardian.com/us-news/2015/jun/09/the-counted-police-killings-us-vs-other-countries.

Leduff, C. 2010. "What Killed Aiyana Stanley-Jones?" November–December 2010. www.motherjones.com/politics/2010/09/aiyana-stanley-jones-detroit/.

Lee, J. 2014. "Exactly How Often Do Police Shoot Unarmed Black Men? The Killing in Ferguson Was One of Many Such Cases." *Mother Jones*. August 15, 2014. www.motherjones.com/politics/2014/08/police-shootings-michael-brown-ferguson-black-men/.

Lewis, V., M. Emerson, and S. Klineberg. 2011. "Who We'll Live with: Neighborhood Racial Composition Preferences of Whites, Blacks, and Latinos." *Social Forces* 89 (4): 1385–407.

Lieberson, S. 1980. *A Piece of the Pie: Blacks and White Immigrants since 1880*. Berkeley: University of California Press.

Lind, D. 2015. "The FBI Is Trying to Get Better Data on Police Killings. Here's What We Know Now." *Vox*. Updated April 10, 2015. www.vox.com/2014/8/21/6051043/how-many-people-killed-police-statistics-homicide-official-black.

Litwack, L. F. 2004. "Hellhounds." In *Violence in War and Peace: An Anthology*, edited by N. Scheper-Hughes and P. Bourgois, 123–28. Malden, Mass.: Blackwell.

Losen, D. J., and G. Orfield. 2002. *Racial Inequity in Special Education*. Cambridge, Mass.: Harvard Education Press.

Lowenstein, J. K. 2007. "Killed by the Cops." *COLORLINES*. November 4, 2007. www.colorlines.com/articles/killed-cops.

Luke, T. 2021. "Democracy under Threat After 2020 National Elections in the USA: 'Stop the Steal' or 'Give More to the Grifter-in-Chief?'" *Educational Philosophy and Theory*.

Mann, E. 2010. "Transformative Organizing." *Race, Poverty, & the Environment* 17 (2):84–87.

Mapping Police Violence. Updated March 31, 2022. www.mappingpoliceviolence.org.

Martinot, S. 2010. *The Machinery of Whiteness: Studies in the Structure of Racialization*. Philadelphia: Temple University Press.

Massey, D. 1990. "American Apartheid: Segregation and the Making of the Underclass." *American Journal of Sociology* 96 (2): 329–57.

———. 2015. "The Legacy of the 1968 Fair Housing Act." *Sociological Forum* 30:571–88.

———. 2017. "Why Death Haunts Black Lives." *Proceedings of the National Academy of Sciences of the United States of America* 114 (5): 800–802.

Massey, D. S., and N. A. Denton. 1988. "Suburbanization and Segregation in U.S. Metropolitan Areas." *American Journal of Sociology* 94 (3):592–626.

———. 1993. *American Apartheid: Segregation and the Making of the Underclass*. Cambridge, Mass.: Harvard University Press.

Massey, D. S., and G. Lundy. 2001. "Use of Black English and Racial Discrimination in Urban Housing Markets: New Methods and Findings." *Urban Affairs Review* 36 (4): 452–69.

Massey, D., and B. Mullan. 1984. "Processes of Hispanic and Black Spatial Assimilation." *American Journal of Sociology* 89 (4): 836–73.

Maxime, Farnel. 2018. "Zero-Tolerance Policies and the School to Prison Pipeline." January 18, 2018. Shared Justice. Center for Public Justice. www.sharedjustice.org/domestic-justice/2017/12/21/zero-tolerance-policies-and-the-school-to-prison-pipeline.

McCardle, A., and T. Erzen, eds. 2001. *Zero Tolerance: Quality of Life and the New Police Brutality in New York City*. New York: New York University Press.

Mearest, T. L. 2015. "Programming Errors: Understanding the Constitutionality of Stop-and-Frisk as a Program Not an Incident." *University of Chicago Law Review* 82 (1): 159–79.

Mendez, D. D., V. K. Hogan, and J. Culhane. 2011. "Institutional Racism and Pregnancy Health: Using Home Mortgage Disclosure Act Data to Develop an Index for Mortgage Discrimination at the Community Level." *Public Health Reports, 1974* 126:102–14.

Meronek, T. 2013. "How Did Kayla Moore Die?" *EBX: East Bay Express*. March 4, 2013. https://eastbayexpress.com/how-did-kayla-moore-die-1/.

Meyerhoffer, C. 2015. "'I Have More in Common with Americans Than I Do with Illegal Aliens': A Cultural Threat Theory of Neighborhood Preferences." *Sociology of Race and Ethnicity* 1 (3): 378–93.

———. 2016. "'A Grain of Salt in a Pepper Shaker': Interviewing Whites, Blacks, and Latinos about their Neighborhood Preferences." *Sociological Forum* 31 (3): 531–54.

———, ed. 2021. *Race: Identity, Ideology, and Inequality*. San Diego: Cognella Academic Publishing.

Meyerhoffer, C., and J. Kenty-Drane. 2018. "Principles of Racial Integration vs. Perceptions of Non-White Neighborhoods: Comparing Hypothetical and Real Neighborhood Choice." *Journal of Urban Affairs* 41(6): 1–16.

Minow, M. 2011. "Confronting the Seduction of Choice: Law, Education, and American Pluralism." *Yale Law Journal* 120(4): 814–48.

Morris, M. 2012. "Race, Gender, and the School-to-Prison Pipeline: Expanding Our Discussion to Include Black Girls." *African American Policy Forum*. October 2012. Retrieved from http://schottfoundation.org/resources/race-gender-and-school-prison-pipeline-expanding-our-discussion-include-black-girls.

———. 2018. *Pushout: The Criminalization of Black Girls in Schools*. New York: New Press.

Muhammad, K. G. 2010. *The Condemnation of Blackness: Race, Crime, and the Making of Modern Urban America*. Cambridge, Mass.: Harvard University Press.

Mullen, S., L. R. Kruse, A. J. Goudsward, and A. Bouges. 2020. "Crack vs. Heroin: An Unfair System Arrested Millions of Blacks, Urged Compassion for Whites." *app. (Asbury Park Press)*. December 2, 2019. www.app.com/in-depth/news/local/public-safety/2019/12/02/crack-heroin-race-arrests-blacks-whites/2524961002/.

National Center for Education Statistics. 1999. *Mini-Digest of Education Statistics 1998* (NCES publication No. 1999–0391). Washington, D.C.: U.S. Department of Education Printing Office.

National Research Council. 2002. "Minority Students in Special and Gifted Education" (Committee on Minority Representation in Special Education, M. S. Donovan, and C. T. Cross, eds., Division of Behavioral and Social Sciences and Education). Washington, D.C.: National Academy Press.

Newport, F. 2013. "In U.S., 24% of Young Black Men Say Police Dealings Unfair." *Gallup*. July 16, 2013. https://news.gallup.com/poll/163523/one-four-young-black-men-say-police-dealings-unfair.aspx.

Nolan, K. 2011. *Police in the Hallways: Discipline in an Urban High School*. Minneapolis: University of Minneapolis Press.

O'Hear, M. M. 2016. "Justice Reinvestment and the State of State Sentencing Reform." *Federal Sentencing Reporter* 29 (1): 1–5.

Oliver, M., and T. Shapiro. 1995. *Black Wealth/White Wealth: A New Perspective on Racial Inequality*. New York: Routledge.

"OLR Research Report." The Connecticut General Assembly. Office of Legislative Research. Accessed July 24, 2022. www.cga.ct.gov/PS94/rpt/olr/htm/94-R-1040.htm

Omi, M., and H. Winant. 1994. *Racial Formation in the United States from the 1960s to the 1990s*. New York: Routledge.

———. 2015. *Racial Formation in the United States*. 3rd ed. New York: Routledge.

Ondrich, J., S. Ross, and J. Yinger. 2000. "How Common Is Housing Discrimination? Improving on Traditional Measures." *Journal of Urban Economics* 47 (3): 470–500.

———. 2003. "Now You See It, Now You Don't: Why Do Real Estate Agents Withhold Available Houses from Black Customers?" *Review of Economics and Statistics* 85 (4): 854–73.

Orfield, G., and C. Lee. 2004. *Brown at 50: King's Dream or Plessy's Nightmare?* Cambridge, Mass.: The Civil Rights Project, Harvard University.

Ortiz, Erik. 2022. "Thousands of Federal Inmates Still Await Early Release under Trump-era First Step Act." *NBC* News. www.nbcnews.com/news/us-news/thousands-federal-inmates-still-await-early-release-trump-era-first-st-rcna35162.

Pallas, A. M., G. Natriello, and E. McDill. 1989. "The Changing Nature of the Disadvantaged Population: Current Dimensions and Future Trends." *Educational Researcher* 18 (5): 16–22.

Parker, L. 2003. "Critical Race Theory in Education: Possibilities and Problems." *Counterpoints* 168:184–98.

Pattillo, M. 2005. "Black Middle-Class Neighborhoods." *Annual Review of Sociology* 31: 305–29.

———. 2007. *Black on the Block: The Politics of Race and Class in the City*. Chicago: University of Chicago Press.

Pattillo-McCoy, M. 1999. *Black Picket Fences: Privilege and Peril among the Black Middle Class*. Chicago: University of Chicago Press.

Paybarah, A., and J. Diaz. 2020. "Protests in Philadelphia after Police Fatally Shoot Black Man." *New York Times*. October 27, 2020, updated October 29, 2020. www.nytimes.com/2020/10/27/us/philadelphia-police-shooting-walter-wallace-jr.html.

Peacher, A. 2016. "There's Another Armed Group in Burns and It's Not the Bundys." *Oregon Public Broadcasting*. January 10, 2016. www.opb.org/news/series/burns-oregon-standoff-bundy-militia-news-updates/theres-another-armed-group-in-burns-and-theyre-not-the-bundys/.

Pfander, J. E. 2011. "Resolving the Qualified Immunity Dilemma: Constitutional Tort Claims for Nominal Damages. *Columbia Law Review* 111 (7): 1601–39.

Phipps, C., and S. Levin. 2016. "Last Oregon Militia Members Say They Will Turn Themselves Over to FBI—as It Happened.". *Guardian* (U.S. edition). Updated February 10, 2016. www.theguardian.com/us-news/live/2016/feb/11/oregon-standoff-escalates-fbi-armed-occupants-malheur-wildlife-refuge-live?filterKeyEvents=false&page=with:block-56bbf8f4e4b00ce1debeaaf9.

Piana, L. D. 2000. *Still Separate. Still Unequal: 46 Years After Brown v. Board of Education* (fact sheet on educational inequality). Oakland, Calif.: Applied Research Center.

Pinto, N. 2012. "Family Sues to Learn Why Shereese Francis Was Suffocated in Her Home by Police." *Village Voice*. June 26, 2012. www.villagevoice.com/2012/06/26/family-sues-to-learn-why-shereese-francis-was-suffocated-in-her-home-by-police/.

Porter, R. E. 1995. "The History of Policing in the United States." In *The Encyclopedia of Police Science*, edited by W. G. Bailey, 114. 2nd ed. New York: Garland.
Provine, D. 2007. *Unequal under Law: Race in the War on Drugs*. Chicago: University of Chicago Press.
Quillian, L. 1995. "Prejudice as a Response to Perceived Group Threat: Population Composition and Anti-immigrant and Racial Prejudice in Europe." *American Sociological Review* 60 (4): 586–611.
Quillian, L., and D. Pager. 2001. "Black Neighbors, Higher Crime? The Role of Racial Stereotypes in Evaluations of Neighborhood Crime." *American Journal of Sociology* 107 (3): 717–67.
Rawick, G. P., ed. 1972. *The American Slave: A Composite Autobiography*. 19 vols. Westport, Conn.: Greenwood. Vol. 9.
Reichel, P. 1999. "Southern Slave Patrols as a Transitional Police Type." In *Policing Perspectives: An Anthology*. Los Angeles: Roxbury.
Robinson, L., and A. Grant-Thomas. 2004. *Race, Place, and Home: A Civil Rights and Metropolitan Opportunity Agenda*. Cambridge: The Civil Rights Project, Harvard University.
Roediger, D. R. 1999. *The Wages of Whiteness: Race and the Making of the American Working Class*. London: Verso.
Rosenbaum, D. 2007. "Police Innovation Post 1980: Assessing Effectiveness and Equity Concerns in the Information Technology Era." *Institute for the Prevention of Crime Review* 1:11–44.
Rosenbaum, J. 1995. "Changing the Geography of Opportunity by Expanding Residential Choice: Lessons from the Gautreax Program." *Housing Policy Debate* 6 (1): 231–69.
Rosenbaum, J., L. Reynolds, and S. Deluca. 2002. "How Do Places Matter? The Geography of Opportunity, Self-efficacy and a Look Inside the Black Box of Residential Mobility." *Housing Studies* 17:71–82.
Rosenzweig, D. 2002. "No Charges in Killing of Tyisha Miller." *Los Angeles Times*. December 13, 2002. www.latimes.com/archives/la-xpm-2002-dec-13-me-tyisha13-story.html.
Rossel, C. 2003. "The Desegregation Efficiency of Magnet Schools." *Urban Affairs Review* 38 (5): 697–725.
Rothkopf, J. 2015. "Fox Legal Analyst: Planting Weapons Used to be 'Standard Operating Procedure' for Cops." April 8, 2015. *Salon*. www.salon.com/2015/04/08/fox_legal_analyst_planting_weapons_used_to_be_standard_operating_procedure_for_cops.
Rothstein, R. 2017. *The Color of Law: A Forgotten History of How Our Government Segregated America*. New York: Liveright.
———. 2019. "The Myth of *de Facto* Segregation." *Phi Delta Kappan* 100 (5): 35–38.
Ruechel, F. 1997. "New Deal Public Housing, Urban Poverty, and Jim Crow: Techwood and University Homes in Atlanta." *Georgia Historical Quarterly* 81 (4): 915–37.
Say Her Name: Resisting Police Brutality Against Black Women. African American Policy Forum and Center for Intersectionality and Social Policy Studies, July 2015 Update. https://static1.squarespace.com/static/53f20d90e4b0b80451158d8c/t/5edc95fba357687217b08fb8/1591514635487/SHNReportJuly2015.pdf. (Note 44 on p. 38 reads, "Frances Garrett, 'Interview on Michelle Cusseaux,' interview by authors, May 17, 2015.")
Schelling, T. 1971. "Dynamic Models of Segregation." *Journal of Mathematical Sociology* 1:143–86.

Schott Foundation for Public Education. "School-to-Prison Pipeline Starts in Preschool." 2016. Accessed July 18, 2022. http://schottfoundation.org/blog/2016/10/24/school-prison-pipeline-starts-preschool.

Semyonov, M., A. Glickman, and M. Krysan. 2007. "Europeans' Preference for Ethnic Residential Homogeneity: Cross-National Analysis of Response to Neighborhood Ethnic Composition." *Social Problems* 54 (4): 434–53.

Shedd, C. 2015. *Unequal City: Race, Schools, and Perceptions of Injustice*. New York: Russell Sage Foundation.

Shester, K. L. 2013. "The Local Economic Effects of Public Housing in the United States." *Journal of Economic History* 73 (4): 978–1016.

Simms, A. 2019. "The 'Veil' of Racial Segregation in the 21st Century: The Suburban Black Middle Class, Public Schools, and Pursuit of Racial Equity." *Phylon* 56 (1):81–110.

Simon, S. 2021. "Understanding the Pushback against Critical Race Theory in Schools." *NPR*. Heard on *Weekend Edition Saturday*. Mp3 (5:49) and transcript. www.npr.org/2021/06/05/1003533656/understanding-the-pushback-against-critical-race-theory-in-schools.

Singal, J. 2014 "White People Think Black People Are Magical." *The Cut*. November 14, 2014. www.thecut.com/2014/11/white-people-think-black-people-are-magical.html.

Sirin, C. V. 2011. "From Nixon's War on Drugs to Obama's Drug Policies Today: Presidential Progress in Addressing Racial Injustices and Disparities." *Race, Gender & Class* 18(3–4):82–99.

Skolnick, J. H. 1966. *Justice without Trial: Law Enforcement in Democratic Society*. New York: Wiley.

Sleeter, C. E. 1993. "How White Teachers Construct Race." In *Race, Identity, and Representation in Education*, edited by C. McCarthy and W. Crichlow, 157–71. New York: Routledge.

Sleeter, C., and P. McLaren. 1995. *Multicultural Education, Critical Pedagogy, and the Politics of Difference*. Albany: State University of New York Press.

Smiley, C. J., and D. Fakunle. 2016. "From 'Brute' to 'Thug': The Demonization and Criminalization of Unarmed Black Male Victims in America." *Journal of Human Behavior in the Social Environment* 26(3–4):350–66.

Smrekar, C. 2009. "Beyond the Tipping Point: Issues of Racial Diversity in Magnet Schools following Unitary Status." *Peabody Journal of Education* 84 (2): 209–26.

Spruill, L. H. 2016. "Slave Patrols, 'Packs of Negro Dogs' and Policing Black Communities." *Phylon* 53 (1): 42–66.

Steinberg, R. G. 2015. "Police, Power, and the Scaring of America: A Personal Journey." *Yale Law and Policy Review* 34 (1): 131–53.

Stevenson, B. 2017. "A Presumption of Guilt: The Legacy of America's History of Racial Injustice." In *Policing the Black Man: Arrest, Prosecution, and Imprisonment*, edited by A. Davis, 3–30. New York: Pantheon.

Smedley, A. 1993 (1999). *Race in North America: Origin and Evolution of a Worldview*. Boulder, Colo.: Westview.

South, S., and K. Crowder. 1997. "Escaping Distressed Neighborhoods: Individual, Community, and Metropolitan Areas." *American Journal of Sociology* 102 (4): 1040–84.

South, S., and G. Deane. 1993. "Race and Residential Mobility: Individual Determinants and Structural Constraints." *Social Forces* 72 (1): 147–67.

Sugrue, T. J. 1996. *The Origins of the Urban Crisis: Race and Inequality in Postwar Detroit*. Princeton, N.J.: Princeton University Press.

Sui, D. Z., and X. B. Wu. 2006. "Changing Patterns of Residential Segregation in a Prismatic Metropolis: A Lacunarity-Based Study in Houston, 1980–2000." *Environment and Planning B: Planning and Design* 33: 559–79.

Swaine, J., O. Laughland, and J. Lartey. 2015. "Black Americans Killed by Police Twice as Likely to Be Unarmed as White People." *Guardian* (U.S. edition). June 1, 2015. www.theguardian.com/us-news/2015/jun/01/black-americans-killed-by-police-analysis.

Swartz, E. 1992. "Emancipatory Narratives: Rewriting the Master Script in the School Curriculum." *Journal of Negro Education* 61:341–55.

Taylor, K. Y. 2019. *Race for Profit: How Banks and the Real Estate Industry Undermined Black Homeownership*. Chapel Hill: University of North Carolina Press.

Thompson, P. J. 2015. "Broken Policing: The Origins of the 'Broken Windows' Policy." *New Labor Forum* 24 (2): 42–47.

Timberlake, J. M. 2000. "Still Life in Black and White: Effects of Racial and Class Attitudes on Prospects for Racial Integration in Atlanta." *Sociological Inquiry* 70 (4): 420–45.

Tolnay, S.E. 2003. "The African American 'Great Migration' and Beyond." *Annual Review of Sociology* 29 (1): 209–32.

Tough, R. 1951. "The Life Cycle of the Home Owners' Loan Corporation." *Land Economics* 27 (4): 324–31.

Turner, K. B., D. Giacopassi, and M. Vandiver. 2006. "Ignoring the Past: Coverage of Slavery and Slave Patrols in Criminal Justice Texts." *Journal of Criminal Justice Education* 17 (1): 181–95.

Turner, M. 1992. "Discrimination in Urban Housing Markets: Lessons from Fair Housing Audits." *Housing Policy Debate* 3 (2): 185–215.

U.S. Dept of Defense. "About." Accessed January 29, 2021. www.defense.gov/About/.

U.S. Department of Education. 2004. *To Assure the Free Appropriate Public Education of All Children with Disabilities: Twenty-Fourth Annual Report to Congress on the Implementation of the Individuals with Disabilities Education Act*. Washington, D.C.: Department of Education.

U.S. Department of Justice Civil Rights Division. 2015. "Investigation of the Ferguson Police Department." March 4, 2015. www.justice.gov/sites/default/files/opa/press-releases/attachments/2015/03/04/ferguson_police_department_report.pdf.

Veklerov, K. 2014. "Leaked Documents Shed New Light on Kayla Moore's In-Custody Death." *Daily Californian*. July 18, 2022. www.dailycal.org/2014/05/07/leaked-documents-shed-new-light-kayla-moore-death/.

Vermeer, M. J. D., D. Woods, and B. A. Jackson. 2020. "Would Law Enforcement Leaders Support Defunding the Police? Probably—If Communities Ask Police to Solve Fewer Problems." *Rand Corporation*. August 2020. www.rand.org/pubs/perspectives/PEA108-1.html.

Vitale, A. S. 2017. *The End of Policing*. London: New Left Books.

Wagmiller, R. 2007. "Race and Spatial Segregation of Jobless Men in Urban America." *Demography* 44 (3): 539–62.

Walker, S. 1980. *Popular Justice*. New York: Oxford University Press.

Watts, I. E., and N. Erevelles. 2004. "These Deadly Times: Reconceptualizing School Violence by Using Critical Race Theory and Disability Studies." *American Educational Research Journal* 41:271–99.

Waytz, A., K. M. Hoffman, and S. Trawalter. 2014. "A Superhumanization Bias in Whites' Perceptions of Blacks." *Social Psychological and Personality Science* 6 (3): 352–59.
Weitzer, R., and S. A. Tuch. 2005. "Racially Biased Policing: Determinants of Citizen Perceptions." *Social Forces* 83 (3):1009–30.
Welch, K., and A. Payne. 2010. "Racial Threat and Punitive School Discipline." *Social Problems* 57 (1): 25–48.
West, K. C. 1994. "A Desegregation Tool That Backfired: Magnet Schools and Classroom Segregation." *Yale Law Journal* 103 (8): 2567–92.
Western, B., and C. Muller. 2013. "Mass Incarceration, Macrosociology, and the Poor." *Annals of the American Academy of Political and Social Science* 647:166–89.
White, S. 2003. "Slavery in the North." *OAH Magazine of History* 17 (3): 17–21.
Wilkes, R., and J. Iceland. 2004. "Hypersegregation in the Twenty-First Century." *Demography* 41 (1): 23–36.
Williams, D., and Collins, C. (2001). "Racial Residential Segregation: A Fundamental Cause of Racial Disparities in Health." *Public Health Reports* (September–October): 404–16.
Williams, H., and P. V. Murphy. 1990. "The Evolving Strategy of Police: A Minority View." No. 13. U.S. Department of Justice, Office of Justice Programs, National Institute of Justice. .
Williams, T., L. Abdennabi, and S. Nezhad. 2019. "Editorial Counterpoint: We Must Look Beyond Police for Community Safety." *Star Tribune*. March 21, 2019. https://www.startribune.com/editorial-counterpoint-we-must-look-beyond-police-for-community-safety/507489092/.
Wilson, J. 2016. "Oregon Militia Threatens Showdown with U.S. Agents at Wildlife Refuge." *Guardian* (U.S. edition). January 3, 2016. www.theguardian.com/us-news/2016/jan/03/oregon-militia-threatens-showdown-with-us-agents-at-wildlife-refuge.
Wilson, W. 1987. *The Truly Disadvantaged: The Inner City, the Underclass and Public Policy*. Chicago: University of Chicago Press.
———. *Change Everything: Racial Capitalism and the Case for Abolition.* Berkeley: University of California Press.
Wright, H. K., and S. Alenuma. 2007. "Race, Urban Schools, and Educational Reform: The Context, Utility, Pros, and Cons of the Magnet Example," *Counterpoints* 306: 211–21.
Yinger, J. 1995. *Closed Doors, Opportunities Lost*. New York: Russell Sage Foundation.
Zhang, G. and N. Zeller. 2016. "A Longitudinal Investigation of the Relationship between Teacher Preparation and Teacher Retention." *Teacher Education Quarterly* 43(2):73–92.
Zubrinsky, C., and L. Bobo. 1996. "Prismatic Metropolis: Race and Residential Segregation in the City of Angels." *Social Science Research* 25: 335–74.

INDEX

abolition movement, 94–102
Adelman, R., 45
Alexander, Michelle, 6–7, 26
Almond, Monica, 57
alternative schools. *See* magnet schools
alt-right politics, 108
American history, 60–61, 106
Anderson, Elijah, 10, 57–58, 73
Anti-Drug Abuse Act (1986), 72
anti-miscegenation laws, 18
assimilation: immigrants and, 17, 32; spatial, 43–44, 45
asthma rates, 61–62

Baldwin, James, 66
Balko, Radley, 20, 80, 83–84
banks, 8, 14, 33, 35–37, 44
Baum, Dan, 71–72
Beger, R. R., 62
behavior: of Black children or students, 4–5, 63–64; criminal, 15, 70, 74–75, 81, 98, 103; racialized, 31; residential preferences and, 45–47
Bellesiles, M. A., 87
Black codes, 24–25
Black Lives Matter (BLM), 3, 11, 89, 92–94, 107
Black neighborhoods, 2, 4, 5, 56, 98; home ownership and, 35–36; policing and surveillance of, 29, 90, 100; property values and, 37–38; residential preferences and, 42–43, 45–48; socioeconomic status and, 44; stereotyping of, 48, 78
Blackness, 21, 78; characterizations of, 5–6, 8, 11, 29, 68–69; transatlantic slave trade and, 13, 16–17
Black Panthers, 84
blockbusting, 33, 37, 38
Blue Lives Matter, 94
bodies, Black, 74–75; controlling, 8, 22; policing, 5, 10–11, 75, 78
Brooks, Rayshard, 95
Brown, Michael, 26–27, 90, 92, 93
Brown v. Board of Education, 10, 51, 54, 60, 62
Bundy, Ammon, 88

Cadora, Erica, 104
Californians United for a Responsible Budget (CURB), 96
canine units, 21, 26–27, 62
capitalism, 21, 23, 99, 100
Carleton, George W., 27–28
Castile, Philando, 88
characterizations of Black people, 2, 8, 29; of communities, 71–72; of men, 5–6, 11, 67, 68, 71; superhuman trope, 68, 69, 78, 90
charter schools, 56–58, 106
children: asthma rates, 62; policing of, 2, 5, 10, 29, 62–63; school segregation and, 4–5, 9, 10; teachers and, 5, 51–52. *See also* students
citizenship, 13–14
civil rights, 24, 25, 58, 71, 76–77
Civil War, 23, 24, 31, 67, 87
Coaston, Jane, 106–7
Coates, Ta-Nehisi, 30
colonialism, 12, 13

"color blindness," 3, 7, 12
community safety, 100–1
Connecticut State Department of Education (CSDE), 59
convict leasing, 66–67
crack epidemic, 72–73, 82, 100
crime rates, 27, 46, 47, 64, 80, 100
criminalization, 69, 96, 98, 108; of Black children, 5, 7, 9, 10, 29, 56, 63; of Black communities, 71–72, 78, 100; of Black men, 6, 67, 68, 71, 74; of Black women, 69–70; of drug offenders, 73, 82; media and, 80–81; punishment and, 100, 101
criminal justice system, 1–2, 7, 28, 73, 89–90, 100; early policy, 2–3; failures of, 103–4, 105; implicit biases within, 74; juveniles and, 10, 64; mental health struggles and, 102; Nixon administration and, 80; police accountability and, 25, 76–77, 85, 87, 92; treatment of Black people within, 6, 8–9, 66–67, 70, 81, 94
critical race theory (CRT), 51, 106–7
Cross, B., 52
Crowder, Kyle, 44, 49
Cullors, Patrisse, 92

Davis, Angela, 1, 94, 98
de facto/de jure segregation, 31, 39, 50
Defense, U.S. Department of, 84
dehumanization, 21, 68, 69–70, 76, 80
Denton, Nancy A., 3, 10, 43
disabilities, 54
divestment and reinvestment: in mental health services, 102; policing and, 78, 94–95, 101, 108; prison system and, 97, 104
Dixon, J., 46
Drakulich, K. M., 93
Dred Scott decision (1857), 14
Drug Enforcement Agency (DEA), 81
drugs. *See* War on Drugs
Du Bois, W. E. B., 94
Duke, K., 68
Durose, M. R., 10, 85

Eberhardt, J. L., 74
Ehrlichman, John, 71–72
Ellen, I. G., 48
Embrick, David, 26
enslavement. *See* slavery
eugenics movement, 18, 19
extrajudicial lynching, 23–25, 32, 68, 92

Fakunle, D., 75
Farley, R., 48
Federal Housing Association (FHA), 35–36, 37–38
Ferguson (Mo.): police force, 26–27; riots, 92
First Step Act (2018), 97
Floyd, George, 89, 90, 94, 95, 107
free Black people, 9, 16, 21, 23–25, 39, 67
fugitive slave laws, 20, 23

Gaither, S. E., 68
Garner, Eric, 76
Garza, Alicia, 92
Gates, Daryl, 83–84
ghettos, 2, 3, 32, 39, 43, 65; iconic nature of, 10–11, 73
Gilmore, Ruth Wilson, 97
girls, Black, 37, 63, 69–70
Goel, S., 77
Goff, P. A., 68
Goldberg, J. A., 77
Goldberg, Zach, 107
Greater Hartford Regional School Choice Office (GHRSCO), 59
Great Migration, 3, 8–9, 31–32, 33, 39
gun culture, 79, 87–89
Gun-Free Schools Act (1994), 63

Hadden, Sally, 25
Harris, D., 47
Harry, B., 54
Hartford (Conn.), 58–60
Hattery, Angela J., 7
Hayes, Chris, 99–100, 103
Hayter, Julian, 61, 106
hegemony, 14, 16, 18
Hirschfield, P. J., 10, 89
Hispanics, 28, 30, 42, 44, 46
home ownership, 9, 75; associations, 8; "castle doctrine" and, 11; loans and mortgages, 35–36, 99; real estate agents, 33, 37–38
Home Owners' Loan Corporation (HOLC), 35
housing acts and policies, 17, 33, 34, 36, 38, 99
housing segregation. *See* public housing; racial-residential segregation
hypersegregation, 2, 11, 31

immigrants, 31–32; European, 15; Irish, 17
incarceration, 69, 92; of children or juveniles, 64, 99–100; definition of "mass," 72; for

drug crimes, 72, 73, 80, 81, 82, 100; justice-reinvestment model and, 104; police practices and, 6–7, 70, 71; public vs. private prisons, 96; rates and demographics, 82, 93, 98–99, 104; reform and releases, 97–98
income, 34, 44, 49; asthma rates and, 61–62; school choice and, 55, 57, 58. *See also* socioeconomic status
industrialization/deindustrialization, 4, 21, 32, 34, 96
inferiority/superiority ideologies, 13, 16, 17, 21–22, 56, 68
Ingersoll, R., 53

Jacobson, M. F., 17
Jim Crow segregation, 6–7, 25, 32–33, 39, 50, 67; policing and, 9, 26
justice-reinvestment movement, 104–5
juvenile justice system, 10, 64

Kaba, Mariame, 98, 99, 101, 102, 103
Kaepernick, Colin, 79
Kang, J., 75
Kerner Commission, 33
King, Martin Luther, Jr., 36
Klingner, J. K., 54
Knopp, Fay Honey, 96
Kraska, P. B., 86
Krysan, Maria, 47, 49
Ku Klux Klan (KKK), 24
Kushner, R., 97

labor: control of, 21; forced, 13, 66–67; shortages, 9–10, 32, 33; wage, 16. *See also* slavery
landowners, 12, 21, 67
Langton, L., 10, 85
Lartey, J., 85
Latinx people, 58, 70, 71, 89; crime and incarceration, 64, 72, 74, 81, 82
Lee, J., 71
Lieberson, S., 46
loans/lending, 14, 33, 35–36, 37–38, 42, 44–45; subprime mortgages, 99
Lundy, G., 33

magnet schools, 54–56, 58–59, 106
Malheur National Wildlife Refuge (Ore.), 88
Martin, Trayvon, 92
Massey, Douglas, 3, 10, 31, 33, 43, 44
May, H., 53, 57
media: coverage on crack use, 72–73; depictions of Black victims, 68, 75; recordings of police brutality, 1, 67, 90, 95; role in Nixon's War on Drugs, 80–81
mental health, 69, 78, 95, 100–2, 105
Merrill, L., 53
militarism/militarization, 10, 40, 79, 83–86, 92, 96, 99; protests and, 90
Minneapolis Police Department, 101
Morris, Monique, 51
Mullan, B., 44

National Guard, 89
Native Americans, 8, 12; enslavement of, 15–16
naturalization rights, 15
neighborhood segregation. *See* Black neighborhoods; racial-residential segregation; White neighborhoods
New Deal, 34–35
New York City, 69, 74, 77, 99
New York Police Department (NYPD), 70, 74
night-watch groups, 20, 23, 25. *See also* slave patrols
Nixon administration, 40, 71–72, 79–82, 84, 98–99
Northeastern states, 22–23, 31, 32, 89

Obama, Barack, 108
Ocasio-Cortez, Alexandria, 41
Ofer, Udi, 97
Omi, Michael, 14, 26, 107
opioid epidemic, 73

Pager, D., 46
perceptions, 8, 57, 84, 86, 87; of Black people, 4, 11, 27, 52, 63, 73–74; media, 75; of neighborhoods, 46, 48, 49; of police, 28–29, 70, 74, 76, 93–94; public, 68, 73
phrenology, 18
place-stratification model, 44–45
police brutality: Baldwin on, 66; Black women and, 69; forced labor and, 66–67; killing rates and shootings, 11, 26–27, 70–71, 76, 77, 90, 92–93, 101–2; mistaken killings, 85–86, 88, 89; Ocasio-Cortez on, 41; protests, 90–91, 95; race and racism and, 25–26, 27–29, 74–75, 89–90; raising awareness of, 94; use of canine units, 26–27
policing: accountability and, 6, 68, 76–77, 87; of

policing (*continued*)
Black children or students, 2, 4, 10, 61, 62–65; of Black communities, 15, 26–28, 29, 39–40, 79; of Blackness or Black bodies, 5–6, 7, 10–11, 75, 78; broken-windows, 40, 75–76, 87; defunding and abolishing, 78, 94–102; distrust or mistrust of, 89, 93–94; drug crimes, 72, 73; fear and, 90; heroic narrative of, 86–87; mental health and, 105; militarization of, 40, 79, 83–86, 90, 99; for protection of White people and neighborhoods, 19, 38–39, 50, 99–100; slave patrols and, 8–9, 20, 24, 25–26; stop and frisk practices, 25, 27, 40, 69, 77–78, 86. *See also* racial profiling
polygenesis, 18
Posse Comitatus Act (1878), 83
poverty, 2, 28, 30, 33, 36, 98; crime and, 76, 101; generational, 31; ghetto, 43; schools and, 53
prison-industrial complex, 6, 11, 80, 81–82, 104; abolition movement, 96–100. *See also* incarceration
property values, 37–38, 47
protests, 36, 90, 92, 95, 105, 107
public housing, 4, 9, 33–35, 39
public-safety funding, 104
public schools, 1–2, 7, 11, 19, 75; charter schools, 56–58; enrollment process, 58–60; environmental factors and, 61–62; magnet schools, 54–56, 59, 106; neighborhood segregation and, 4–5, 10, 52–53, 65; policing and, 29, 63; privatized, 99; punitive discipline policies, 63–64; reinvestment in, 78; special education programs, 54; teachers and curricula, 5, 10, 51–52, 53, 60–61, 105–7. *See also* school-to-prison pipeline
Public Works Administration (PWA), 34

qualified immunity, 76–77
Quillian, L., 46

race, constructions of, 13–15; biological and social definitions, 8, 9, 14, 16, 18–19, 107
racial and implicit biases, 47, 56, 58, 73–75, 81; policing and, 70, 77–78, 93
racial hierarchy, 8, 15–16, 18–19, 25; White supremacy and, 12, 14, 67, 94, 108
racial inequality, 1, 2, 7, 15, 72, 89; scholarship and publications on, 3, 41, 43
racial profiling, 69, 89, 93; drug crimes and, 81; linguistic profiling, 33; stop and frisk practices, 27, 40, 77
racial projects, 14–15, 107–8
racial-residential segregation, 3–4, 8, 32, 69, 102; environmental and health factors of, 62; government policy and, 50; individual preferences and, 45–48; mortgage lending discrimination and, 35–36; persistence of, 10, 41–43, 49; policing and, 29, 39–40, 50, 100; property values and, 37–38; public schools and, 4–5, 10, 65; socioeconomic status and, 43–44, 49, 82; state-sanctioned violence and, 38–39; stereotypes and, 6, 48. *See also* public housing
racism, 32, 33, 46, 67, 75, 98; classism and, 99; individual, 12; policing and, 26, 28 70–71, 89; public school curricula and, 60–61, 106; scientific, 17–19; systemic or institutional, 1, 2, 3, 5, 30, 44–45, 63, 106. *See also* White supremacy
raids, 84–86, 90; U.S. Capitol attack, 88–89
rape, 99, 104
real estate sector, 33, 35, 36, 37, 44–45, 75
Reconstruction, 6, 9, 23–25, 27, 68; Du Bois's essay on, 94; government policy and, 31
redlining, 8, 33, 35, 38
Regional School Choice Office (RSCO), 59–60
republican motherhood, 18
residential segregation. *See* Black neighborhoods; racial-residential segregation; White neighborhoods
restorative justice, 103–4
Rodriguez, D., 98
Rogers, Jeff, 83
Rothstein, R., 50, 61–62

school-choice movement, 7, 55–56, 58–60, 99
school curricula, 5, 10, 51–52, 53; CRT and antiracist, 60–61, 105–7; in magnet schools, 54–55
School Resource Officers (SROs), 10, 29, 62, 64, 78
schools. *See* public schools
school-to-prison pipeline, 2, 4–5, 7, 10, 29, 62–63
self-defense, 64, 86, 88
Shedd, Carla, 6, 56, 58
Simon, S., 61
Sirin, C., 81
Skolnick, Jerome, 6
slave patrols: disbandment of, 23–24; history and

ideology, 2–3, 21–23, 39; modern policing and, 8, 19, 20, 24, 25–26, 67
slavery, 12, 13, 67, 69, 108; depictions of Black men and, 5–6; fugitive slaves, 3, 9, 20, 21, 88; illegalization or end of, 19, 23, 27, 32–33, 66; racial hierarchy and, 15–16; rebellions, 20, 22, 103; scientific racism and, 17–18; ships and, 16; southern vs. northern, 22–23
slums, 34
Smart Justice, 97
Smiley, C. J., 75
social mobility, 3, 9, 10, 32, 41; Black communities and, 36, 82, 98
socioeconomic status, 35, 36, 38, 41–42; quality education and, 60, 75; residential preferences and, 46, 47–48, 49; spatial assimilation and, 43–44
South, S., 44
southern states, 4, 9, 22, 25, 32, 66–67
spatial-assimilation model, 43–44
special education programs, 52, 53, 54
Stanley-Jones, Aiyana Mo'nay, 86
Steinberg, Robin G., 86–87
stereotypes, 2, 26, 68, 74, 84; of Black girls, 63; drug crimes and, 80; residential segregation and, 6, 48, 78; of urban schools, 52–53. *See also* characterizations of Black people
Sterling, Alton, 88
stop and frisk practices, 25, 27, 40, 69, 77–78, 86
students, 51–54, 65; academic achievement gap, 56, 57, 58, 62; behavior, 4–5, 62, 63–64; classroom segregation, 55–56; transportation for, 59–60
suburban neighborhoods, 39, 43–44, 46, 90; schools in, 55, 59
Swartz, E., 51
SWAT teams, 10, 83–85
Symbionese Liberation Army (SLA), 84

Taylor, Breonna, 86, 89, 90
teachers and teacher educators, 51–52, 61, 63, 75; shortages and turnover, 53
Teach for America (TFA), 53
technical high-school system schools, 59
terrorism prevention, 84
Terry stops, 40. *See also* stop and frisk practices
Tometi, Opal, 92
transformative organizing, 102–3
Trump, Donald, 88, 107–8
Tuch, S. A., 93–94
Tucker, Susan, 104

United States Housing Authority (USHA), 34
urban schools, 52–53, 55, 56, 59; closure of, 58; surveillance in, 64
U.S. Capitol (D.C.), 88–89
U.S. Constitution: Second Amendment, 88; 13th Amendment, 23, 66; 14th Amendment, 24, 62, 77
U.S. military, 83, 86

Vera Institute of Justice, 64, 105
Vermeer, M. J. D., 95, 105
Veterans Administration (VA), 35–36
victims, 102; Black and Brown people as, 68–69, 75, 78; criminal justice system and, 70; drug addicts as, 73; Latinx and White people as, 81; of police killings, 86, 89–90
violence, 12, 75, 78, 89, 92, 100; canine, 21; characterizations of Black men and, 6, 68; drug crimes and, 72, 81; against police, 94; of slave patrollers, 21, 22, 26; student, 52; toward Black women and girls, 69–70; White mob, 23–25, 32, 38–39, 50. *See also* police brutality

Walker, Kenneth, 86
Wallace, Walter, Jr., 101–2
War on Drugs, 6, 7, 11, 69; crack use and, 72–73; implications for Black communities, 82, 98; incarceration and, 82, 98–99; media coverage, 80–81; Nixon's campaign, 39–40, 71–72, 79–80, 98; racial profiling and, 81
wealth, 36–37, 99
weapons, 63, 74, 87–89, 90
Weitzer, R., 93–94
White/Black binary, 8, 13, 16–17, 61
White flight, 9, 37–38, 39, 106
White neighborhoods: home ownership and, 35–37; keeping Black people out of, 9, 19, 30, 38–39, 50; real estate agents and property values, 33, 37–38, 47; residential preferences and, 42–43, 45–48; schools and, 57; socioeconomic status and, 44, 49
Whiteness, 8, 10, 14, 57; designations and epochs of, 16–17; identity, 16, 17, 19, 107; of public-school curricula, 51, 60, 61
White supremacy, 56, 105, 106; KKK and vigilante

White supremacy (*continued*)
groups, 9, 23–25; origins, 12, 13–14, 67; racial purity and, 18–19; upholding and perpetuating, 6, 7–8, 20, 22, 26, 29, 40, 108
Wilkerson, Isabel, 12
Williams, T. L., 101
Wilson, Darren, 92
Wilson, William Julius, 43
Winant, Howard, 14, 26, 107
women: dehumanization of, 69–70, 76; prison abolition movement and, 96; public school teachers, 5, 10, 51, 52; violence toward, 6, 99–100
World War I, 9, 32
World War II, 32, 34, 36, 66

Yanez, Jeronimo, 88
Yinger, J., 45

Zare, Howard, 103
zero-tolerance drug policies, 7, 29, 69
Zimmerman, George, 92

Printed in the USA
CPSIA information can be obtained
at www.ICGtesting.com
CBHW020219040924
14086CB00025B/447

9 780820 364230